PLYMOUTH'S MILITARY HERITAGE

Ernie Hoblyn

AMBERLEY

First published 2024

Amberley Publishing
The Hill, Stroud
Gloucestershire, GL5 4EP

www.amberley-books.com

Logo source material courtesy of Gerry van Tonder

ISBN 978 1 3981 2032 7 (print)
ISBN 978 1 3981 2033 4 (ebook)

British Library Cataloguing in Publication Data.
A catalogue record for this book is available from the British Library.

Origination by Amberley Publishing.
Printed in Great Britain.

Contents

Introduction

Plymouth is a naval city – everyone knows that. Hundreds of naval ships have been based here. Over the centuries Devonport and its sailors have enjoyed the city's facilities, for good or ill, whilst on leave. The only problem is that ships, although technically based here, spent most of their time elsewhere in the world. Strange as it may seem, the vast majority of local historic military artefacts are actually related to the army.

Looking at the military history of the area around Plymouth, we see various waves of advances in the technology of war. Early cannons had a useful accurate range in the hundreds of yards, so defences had to be built where they could drop cannonballs onto passing ships. By the Second World War it would have been possible for a German battleship to anchor near the Eddystone and bombard Plymouth and its dockyard from there, so defences had to be built capable of hitting ships at that range. Air warfare was unknown in the nineteenth century, but, as we are painfully aware, it was the city's major problem during the Second World War.

In addition to these technological waves there were also political waves, caused by whatever wars and political disagreements were going on in the world at the time. Looking at a list of wars involving England since 1500, there were not many years when we weren't at war with someone – usually the French, but often the Spanish and occasionally the Dutch. Unfortunately, by the time something was built it was quite often obsolete, so many local structures may not have been used or they may have been used and found not to be effective. That is the nature of defence.

Because of this vast expenditure on defences, whether used or not, we have a lot of local places that tell their story, many of which are new to me and possibly to you as well. While I am not an expert in any field I have tried to find out everything I can about them, but inevitably there will be some I know little about, for which I apologise. Things were built, tried and abandoned in wartime with few, if any, records kept, which has made research challenging. However, I have done my best to put them all in some kind of context. Join me on a journey through Plymouth's military heritage.

1. The Normans to the Plantagenets

The earliest military artefacts in the Plymouth area are two ancient castles. The first dates from Norman times. Plympton Castle was built around 1100 either by Richard de Redvers, Earl of Devon or his son Baldwin. It is a classic old castle with a shell keep and it is situated in the heart of Plympton St Maurice.

Originally constructed as a Norman earth and timber motte-and-bailey fortification, Plympton Castle was built in 1136 by Baldwin de Redvers. It was burnt later in the reign of King Stephen and rebuilt but then besieged again in the reign of Henry III (1207–72). By the thirteenth century it had been rebuilt as a circular stone keep on top of the motte, similar in construction to Launceston Castle.

It was owned by the Courtenay family from the time of Henry III until 1539, by which time it was no longer used, but it was reactivated at the start of the Civil War. Prince Maurice, nephew of Charles I, used the castle as his headquarters during the Royalist siege of Plymouth, which supported Parliament. Prince Maurice abandoned Plympton Castle in 1644.

The second artefact is Plymouth Castle. Work is said to have commenced in around 1339. In 1416 two towers were added and in 1519 the defences were further strengthened. To protect the growing settlement, Plymouth's town walls were also started around this time, although a map dated 1540 shows the circuit as still incomplete. Robert Adams made a report to the privy council in 1592 recommending the construction of a modern and effective wall to provide protection to the town. The town walls were shown as complete on a 1643 map. In 1540, Leland, in his *Itinerary*, described 'a castle quadrate, having at each corner a great round tower'. The castle was largely demolished in 1665 to provide material for the Citadel.

The remains of the tower and walls are Grade II listed. All that remains is a tower, with a small section of wall on each side in a cul-de-sac off Lambhay Hill overlooking the Barbican in Plymouth. The tower that survives was possibly a turret of the gatehouse or perhaps an internal tower within the castle.

The only time that Plymouth was invaded was in 1403 – technically just beyond the reign of the Plantagenets. French invaders had sailed into the Sound in 1339 during the Hundred Years' War, sinking some ships and sacking some houses on shore. Then, in 1403, the French landed along the coast and attacked the area north of Sutton, now Exeter Street. They burned many houses and stayed overnight but left the next day. This is the reason that Plymouth had a fear of French invasion for centuries afterwards.

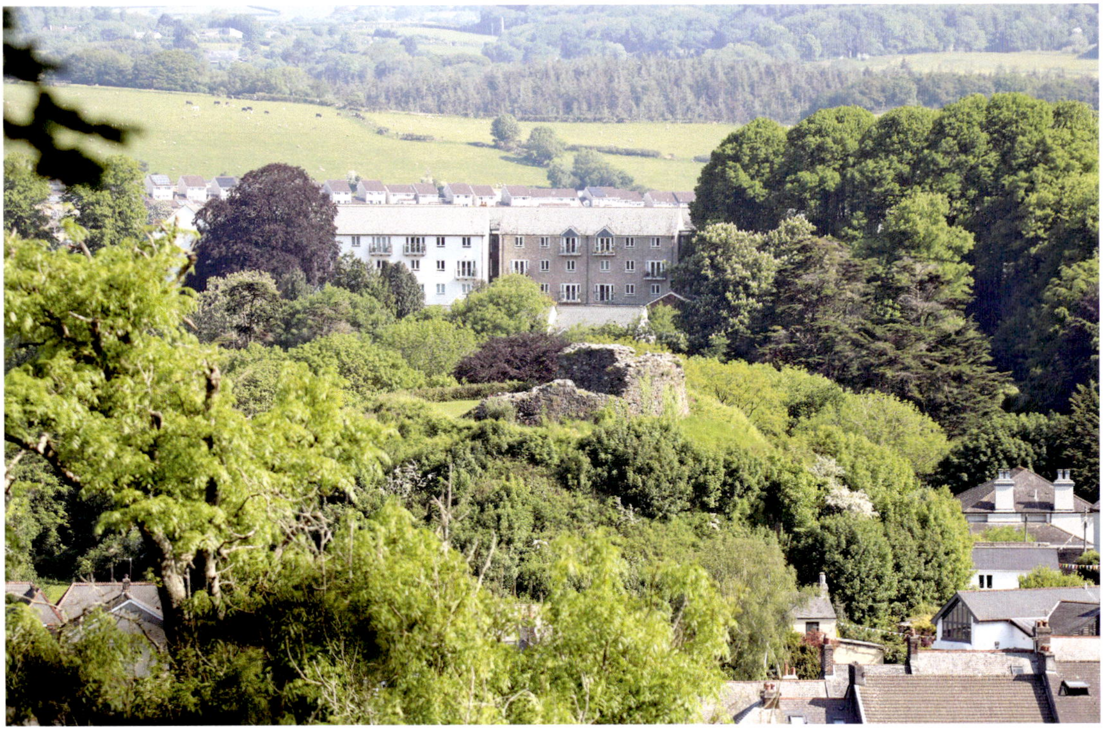

Plympton Castle.

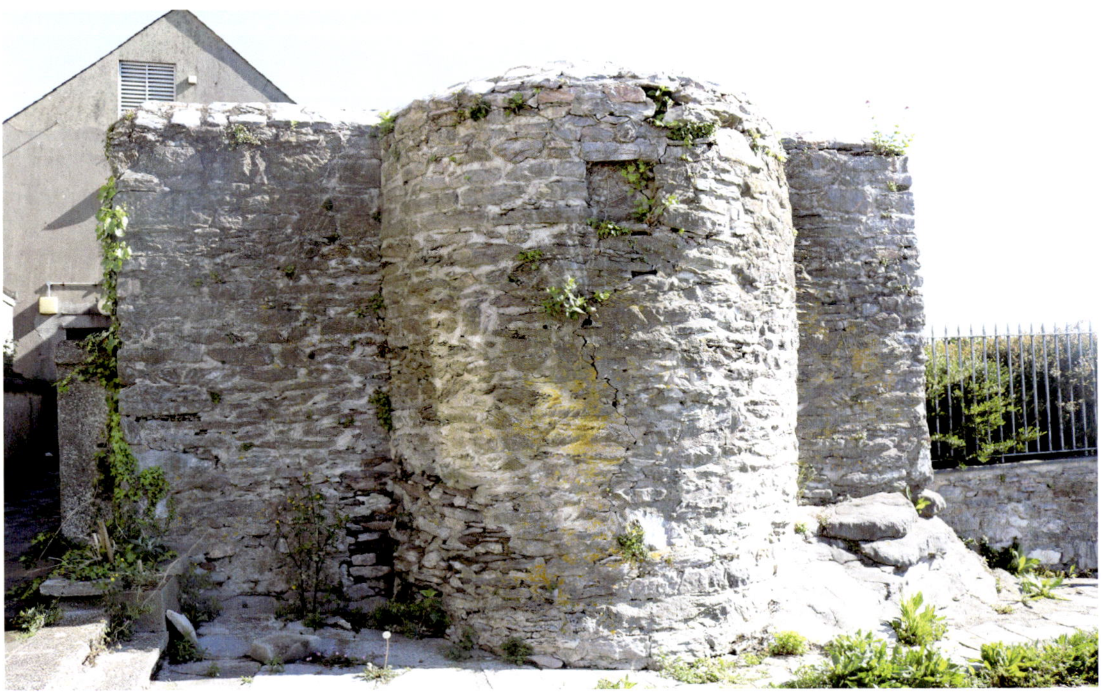

Plymouth Castle.

2. Sixteenth Century: Henry VIII and Elizabeth I

If I may quote again from *The Itinerary of John Leland in or about the Years 1535–1543*:

> The mouth of the gulph wherin the shippes of Plymmouth lyith is waullid on eche side and chainid over in tyme of necessite. On the south west side of this mouth is a blok house: and on a rokky hille hard by it is a stronge castel quadrate having at eche corner a great rounde tower. It semith to be no very old peace of worke.

Here he describes part of the sea defences of Plymouth at that time. Henry VIII had ordered a series of blockhouses to be built along the south coast of England to protect against possible French attacks. Sir Richard Edgcumbe had built a line of blockhouses, both to comply with the king's orders and to protect his own properties in East and West Stonehouse. Starting with the blockhouse in his formal gardens at Mount Edgcumbe, there was a matching one at Devil's Point, the Artillery Tower at Firestone Bay, two more on each side of the entrance to Millbay (now long gone) and finally one on Fisher's Nose at the entrance to Sutton Harbour. Above the latter was of course Plymouth Castle, the 'stronge castel quadrate' Leland referred to.

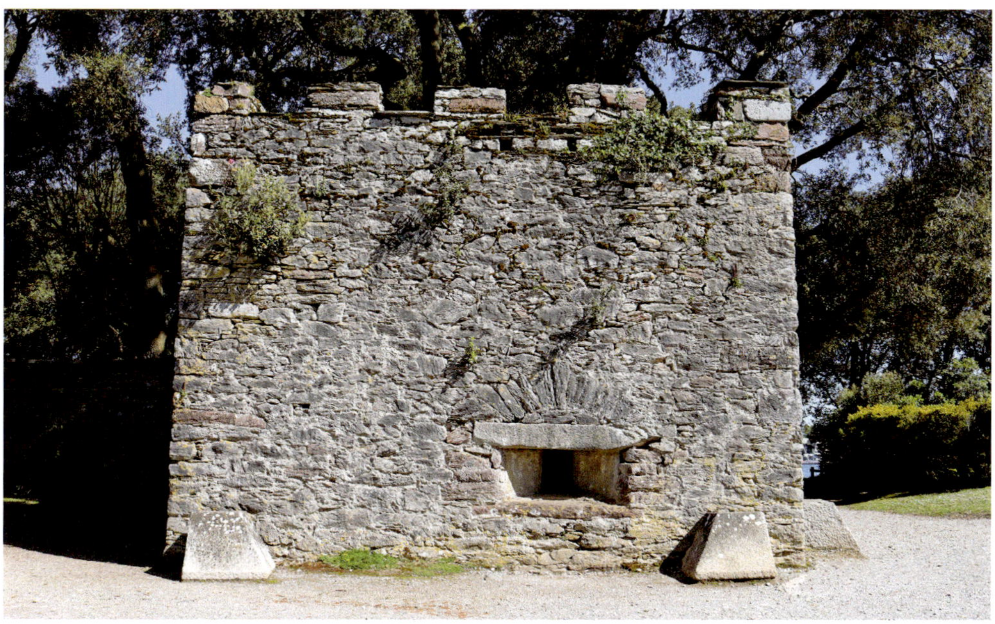

Mount Edgcumbe Blockhouse.

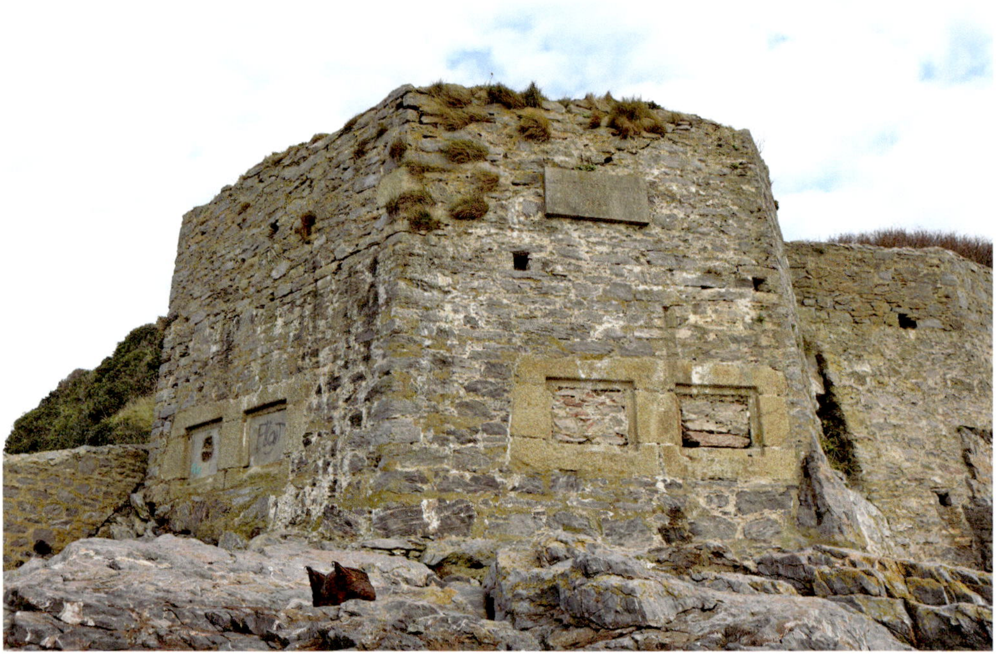

Devil's Point Blockhouse.

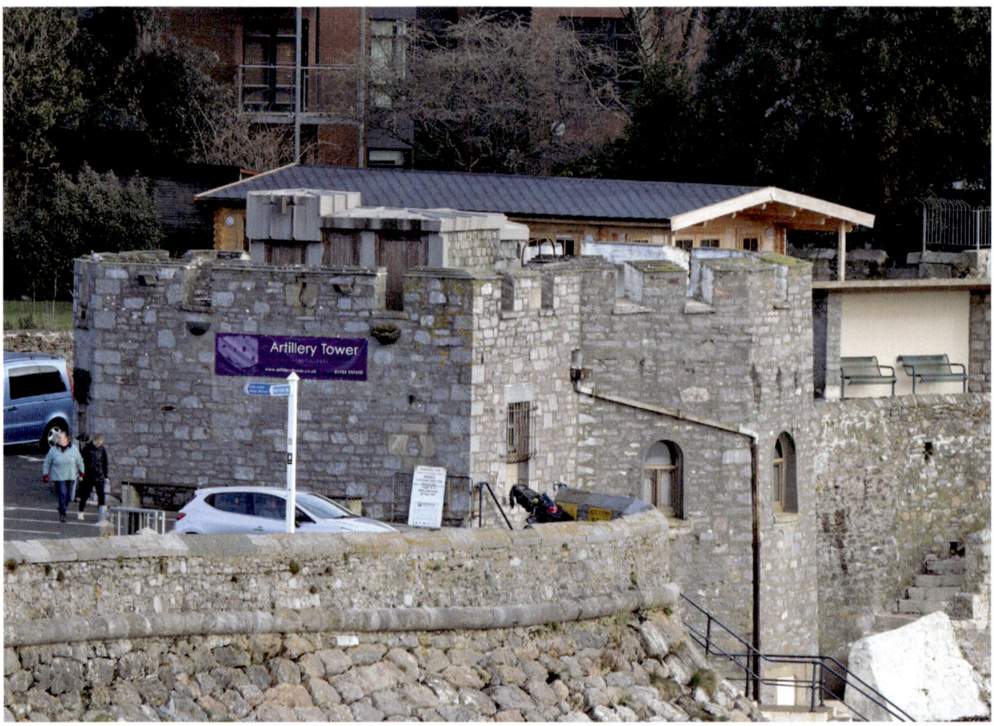

Artillery tower.

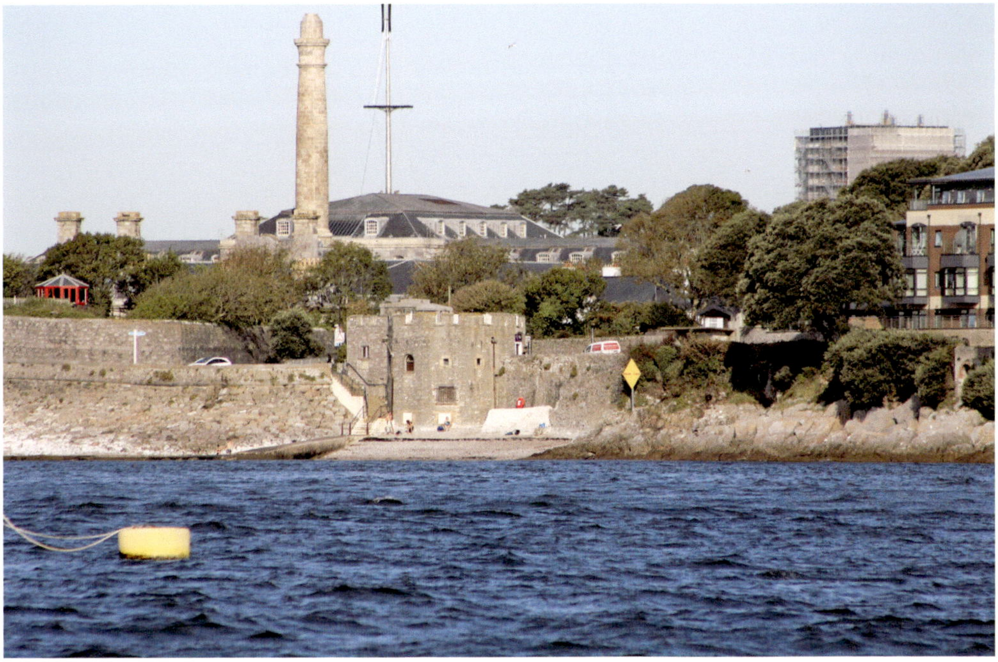

Artillery tower from Drake's Island.

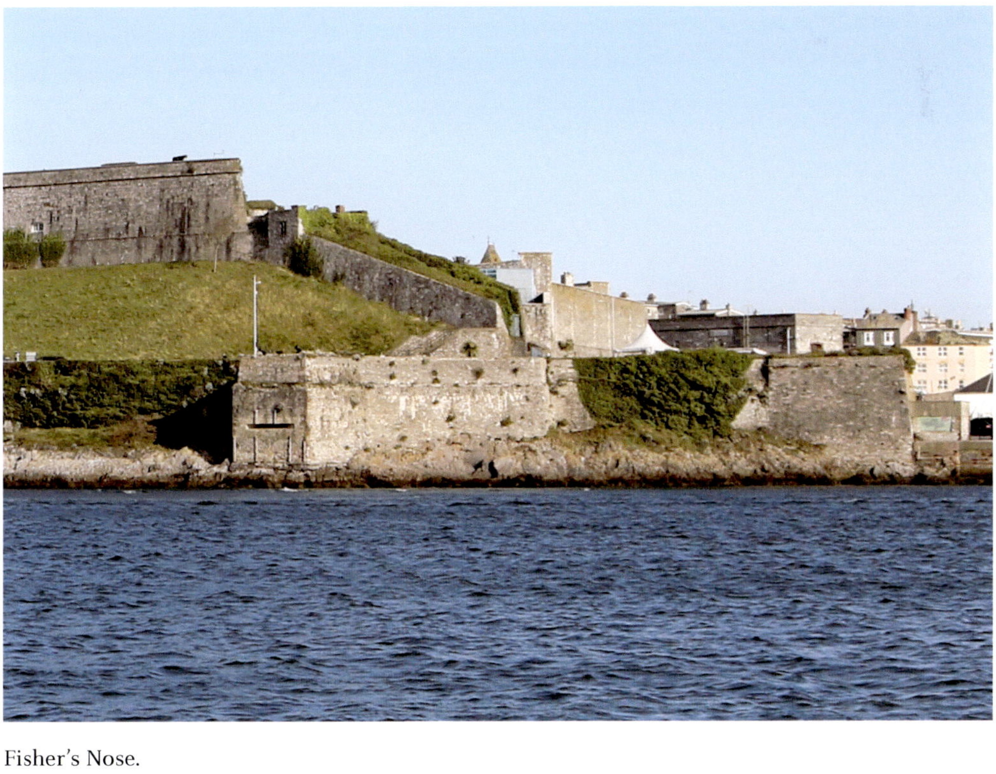

Fisher's Nose.

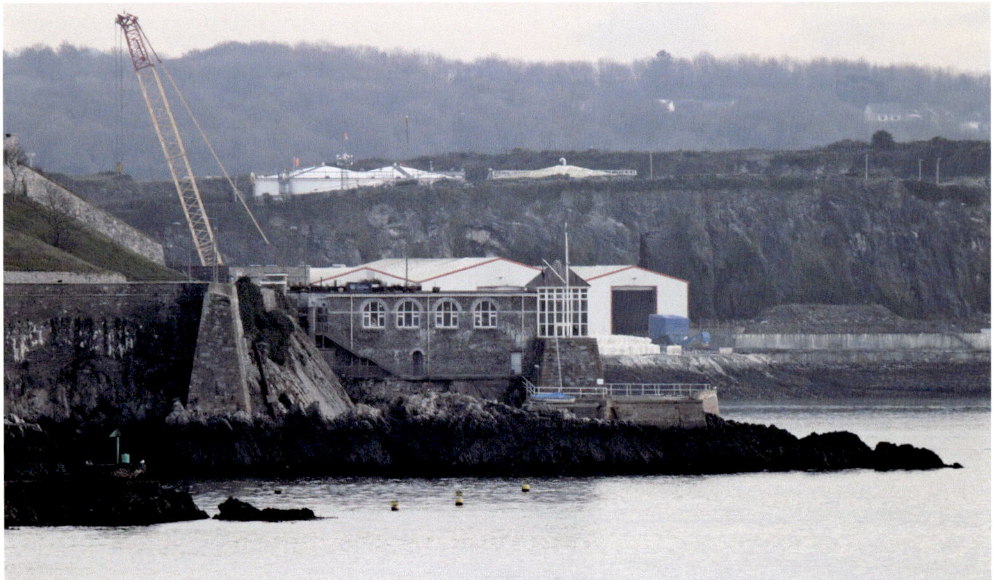

Fisher's Nose from Devil's Point.

The reason for all these blockhouses was to protect the entrances to the various harbours. Given the lack of range and accuracy of the sixteenth-century cannon (it was only accurate to some 300–400 metres), the only way to protect Plymouth's harbours was to have cannon mounted on each side of the entrance to each harbour. Hence the line of Tudor blockhouses that were built along the seafront, allowing any invading ships to be bombarded from each side with some chance of actually doing some damage. Each blockhouse had ports that would have allowed three cannon to fire from it. Given the lack of manoeuvrability of Tudor-era sailing ships, which were entirely dependent on wind direction, it would have taken a very confident (or foolhardy!) captain to sail into such confined waters, let alone those with cannon on either side. Those at Mount Edgcumbe and Devil's Point could fire on ships attempting to enter the Hamoaze and they could also pull a chain between them to block the harbour for ships 'in tyme of necessite' as Leland describes. The Artillery Tower was presumably to prevent an enemy landing at Firestone Bay (and protect Edgcumbe lands at East Stonehouse!). The surviving blockhouses are now listed buildings.

Further fortifications, presumably earth and timber, were also built during the Tudor period. In 1551 St Nicholas' (later Drake's) Island, which had long been in use by the Crown as a customs facility and was fortified at the Crown's expense.

Plymouth increasingly hosted large numbers of privateers and naval ships. Upon the outbreak of war between England and Spain in 1588, Sir Francis Drake sailed from the town to defeat the first great Armada (having famously finished his game of bowls first). Later, Drake pushed for further fortifications to protect Plymouth Sound, leading to the construction of Drake's Fort on the Hoe in 1596. This was predominantly an earth and timber structure and incorporated the earlier blockhouse at Fisher's Nose.

A small artillery battery was also built on Staddon Heights, overlooking Bovisand Bay, to protect its anchorage adjacent to a freshwater stream. This was Staddon Battery, which was constructed on the cliffs overlooking the Sound. Little is known about this early structure and the precise date it was founded is uncertain. However, it was shown on a map dated 1587. It has since been demolished and is now the site of Staddon Cottage.

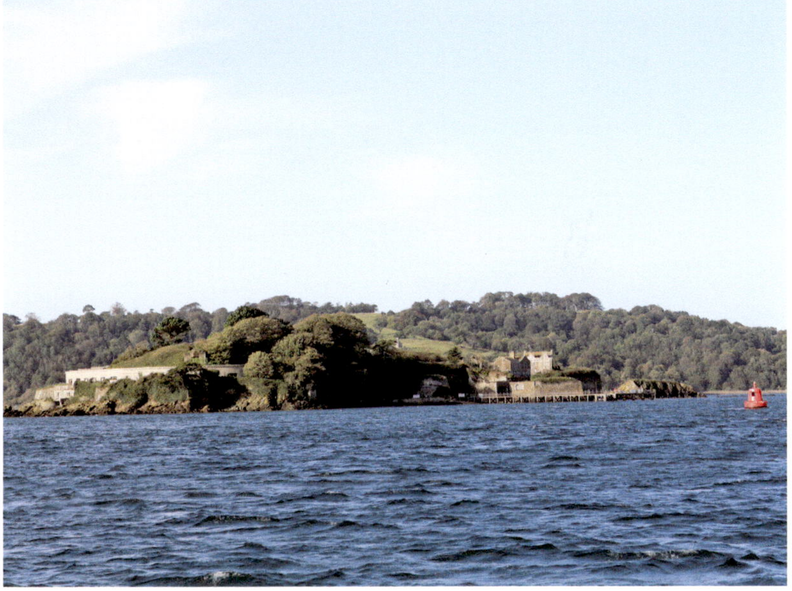

Drake's Island.

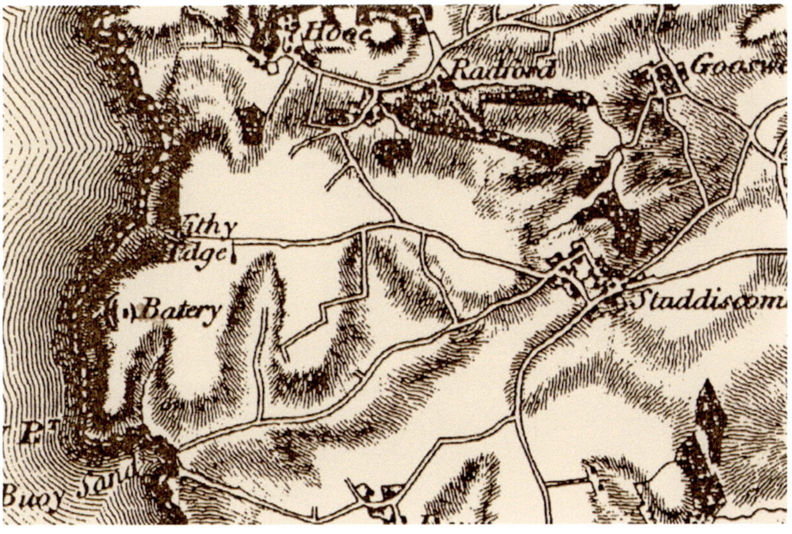

Staddon 'Batery' shown on an 1809 map of Saltram.

3. Seventeenth Century: The Stuarts

Unusually for the south-west, Plymouth supported Parliament in the Civil War. Mount Edgcumbe was a Royalist bastion, so strong defences were needed. As part of Plymouth's defences at this time an outer line of earthworks was constructed along the northern ridge, running west to east from Stonehouse Creek to Lipson, thus overlooking the two valleys that almost bisect Plymouth. A series of earthwork artillery forts was added to this line: Newworke Fort, Penycomquic Fort, Maudlyn Fort, Holiwell Fort and Lipson Fort. These forts have now been buried under modern developments – see the 1643 map here, which also shows the city walls completed as previously mentioned.

After the Civil War these earthwork defences were demolished. However, peace did not last. With England bankrupt after years of war, Parliament attempted to rebuild the country's wealth by implementing the Navigation Acts. These imposed a monopoly on English colonies, prohibiting them from trading with ships from any nation other than England. The Dutch, who relied upon trade with the colonies, declared war. To protect Sutton Pool, Mount Batten Tower was built during the Commonwealth, around 1652, on the site of a Civil War earthwork battery.

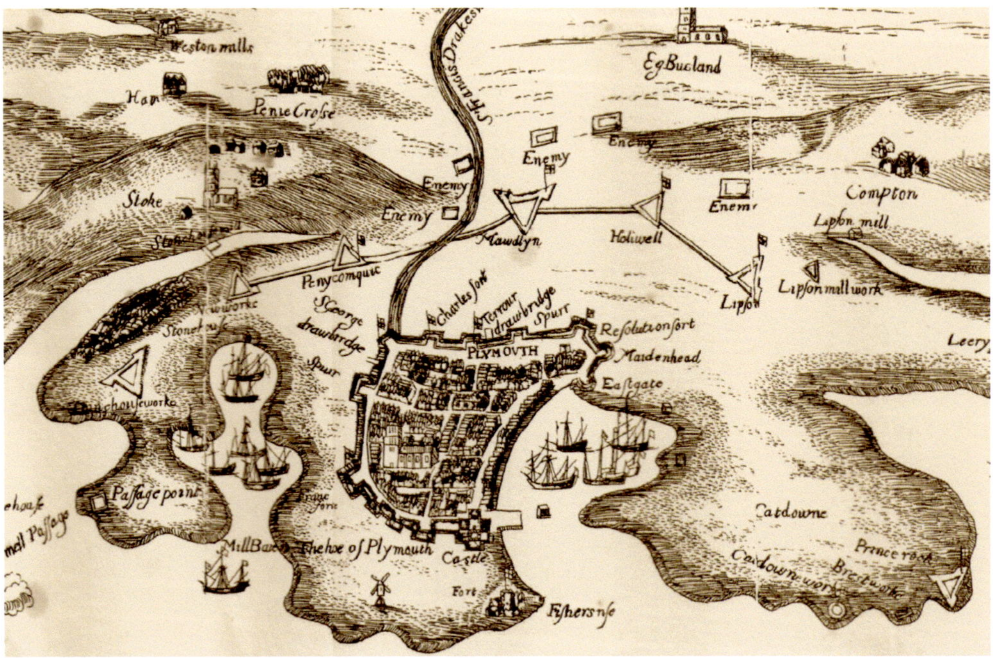

Map from 1643.

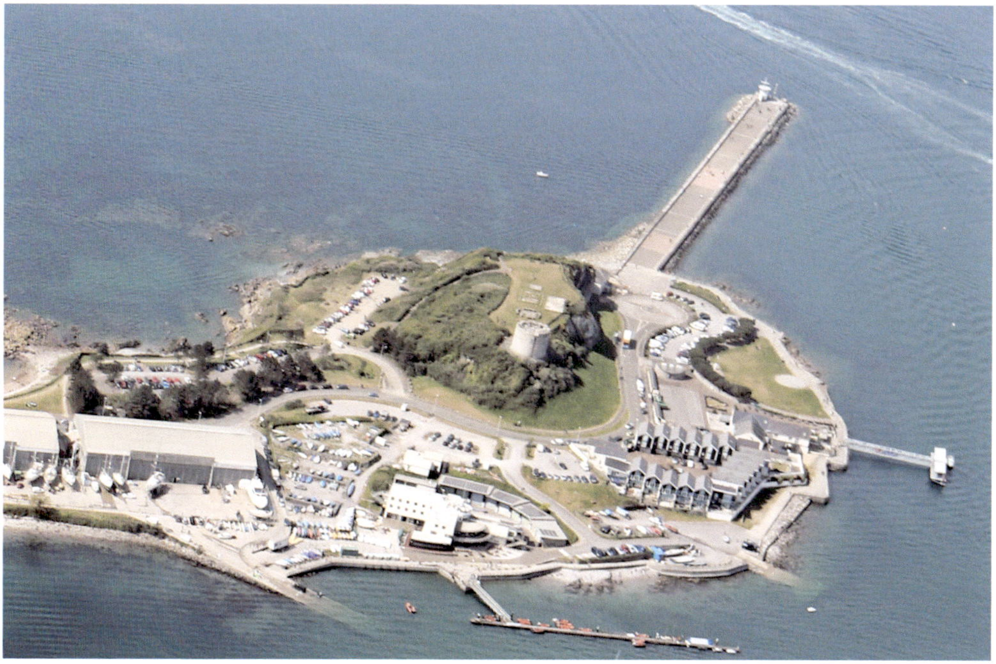

Mount Batten Tower from the air.

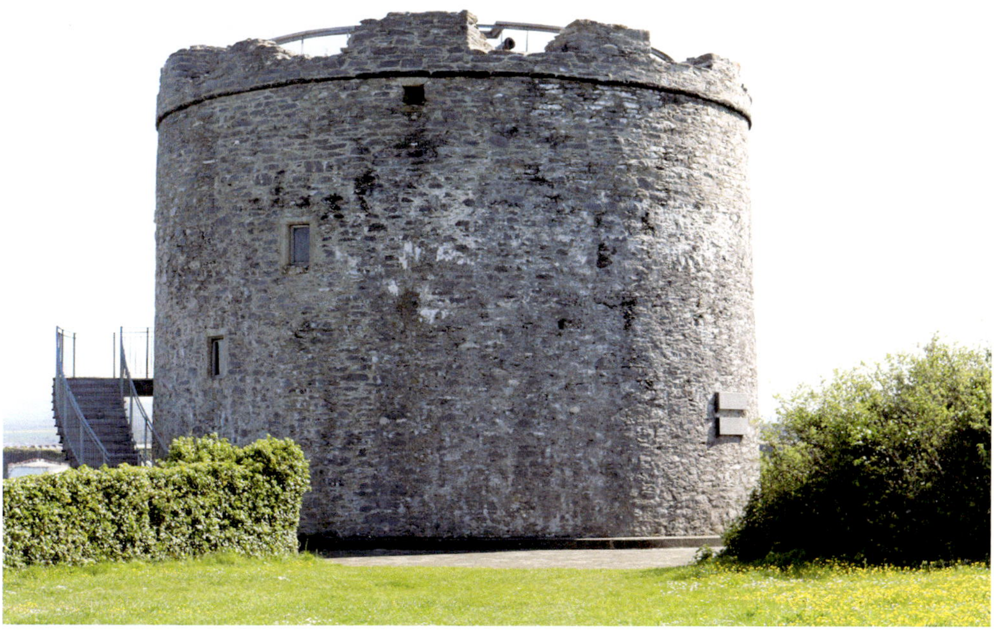

Mount Batten Tower with one cannon visible.

This round artillery tower, when paired with Drake's Fort on the Hoe and Drake's Island, provided extra protection for Sutton Harbour. Periodic warfare continued with the Dutch after the Restoration of the Monarchy, leading to Charles II replacing Drake's Tudor fort with the Royal Citadel. Building work commenced in 1665 with the required land simply being seized by the Crown. Soldiers from the Duke of Cornwall's Regiment were used for construction and by June 1667 the bulwarks had been built to a height of around 12 metres. In that same year a Dutch fleet sailed up the Medway and captured or sank most of the naval ships moored there. This was a major embarrassment for Charles II and caused the diarist Samuel Pepys to write: 'I do fear so much that the whole kingdom is undone, that I do this night resolve to study with my father and wife what to do with the little that I have in money by me.' There were very real fears that the Dutch might have taken London.

The new fortification was significantly larger than Drake's Fort. Ironically, it was a Dutch-born engineer, Sir Bernard de Gomme, who designed the structure. The northern section of the fort was built to a contemporary design, with a deep dry ditch fronting a tall stone curtain wall topped with earth to absorb artillery shot. Three angled bastions projected forward into the ditch, ensuring all sections of the wall could be covered by artillery fire, and an angled ravelin guarded the entrance. The southern section was less conventional as it incorporated both a dedicated harbour to support the Citadel and the still-effective artillery works at the Fisher's Nose in what became known as the Lower Fort.

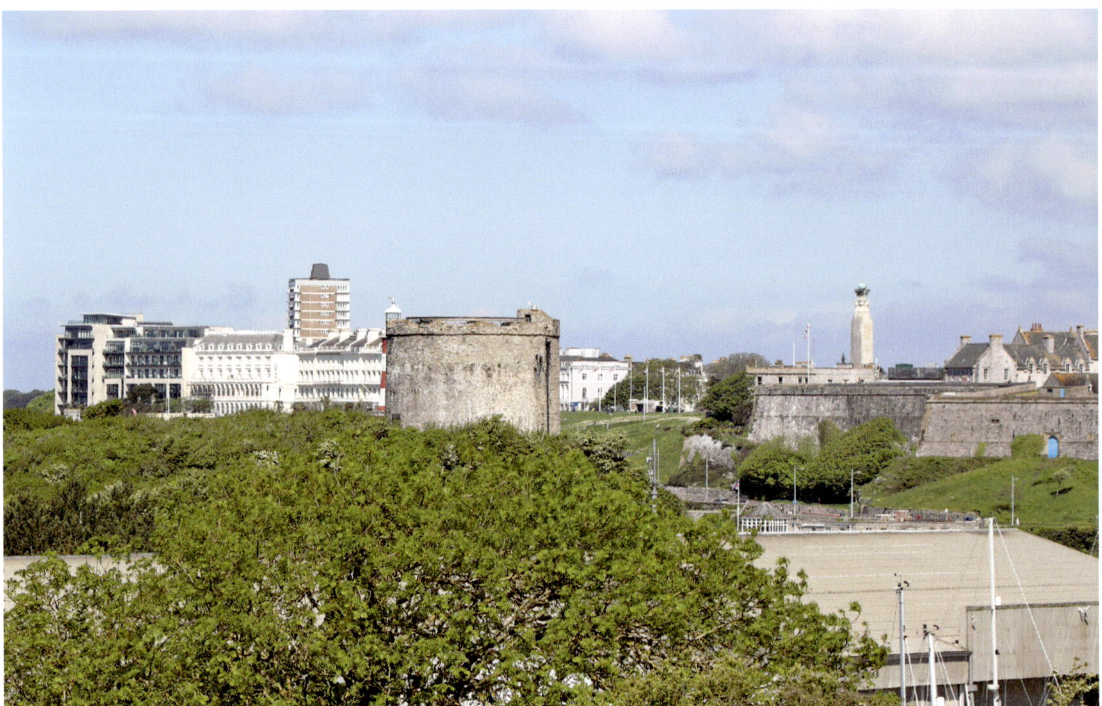

Mount Batten tower with Citadel in background.

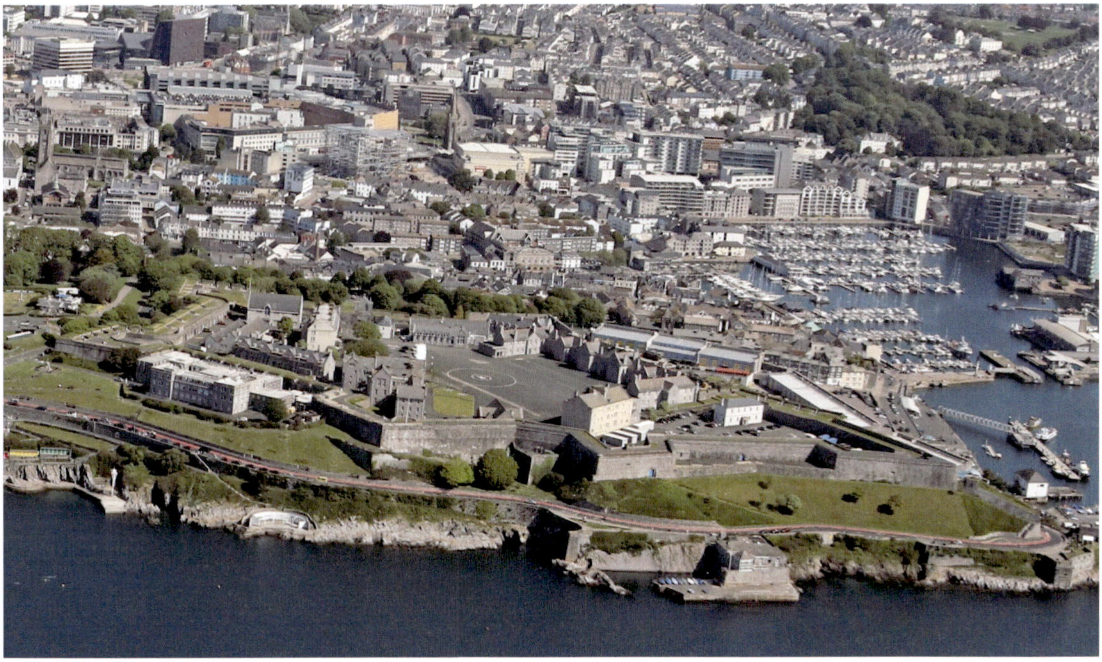

Citadel from the air.

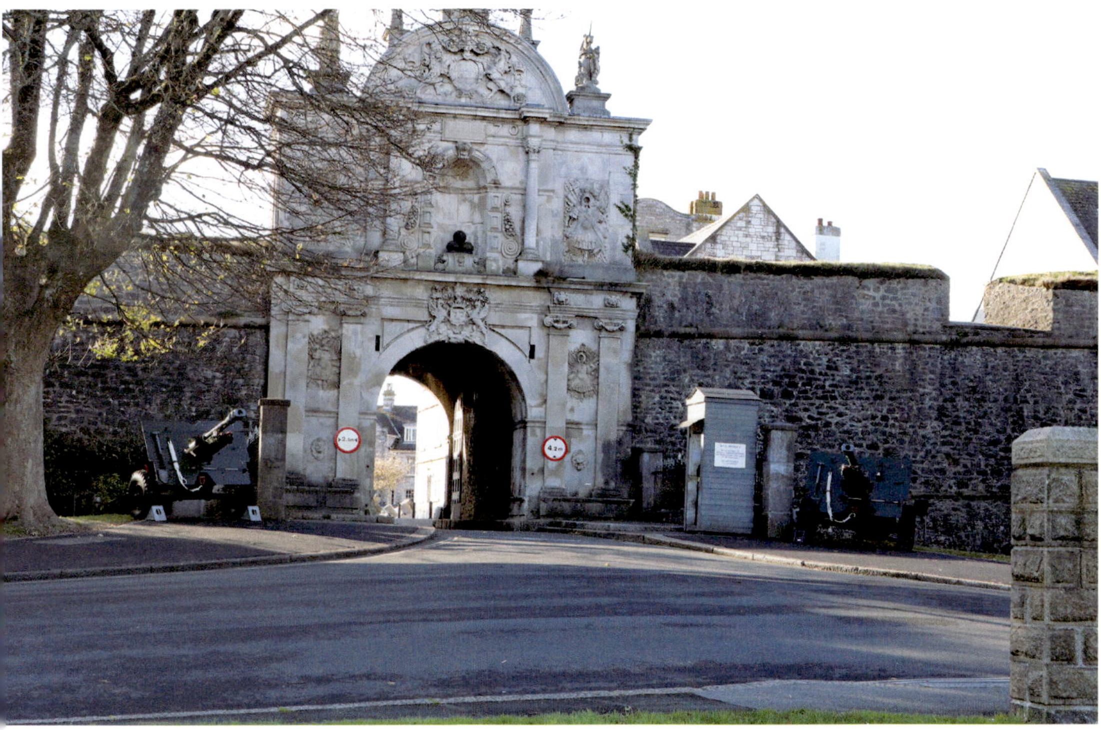

Citadel entrance.

The walls of the Citadel were built from limestone, some quarried from the ditch, whilst granite from Dartmoor was used for dressing. This new structure, built directly over Drake's Fort and incorporating much of the stone from it, was large enough to hold a substantial garrison and had artillery covering the harbour. There is also the lovely – but false – story that Charles had extensive artillery facing towards Plymouth – perhaps indicative of a king who hadn't quite forgiven the town for the staunch Parliamentary support throughout the Civil War. In fact, there are cannon ports all round – a fort with all the guns on one side would be easy to storm!

Queen Anne's Battery was also established at this time, on the east side of Sutton Harbour.

Towards the end of the Stuart period, William III ordered the building of a new dock on the Hamoaze near Plymouth. Started in the early 1690s, by 1700 it was described as 'the latest thinking in the planning and layout of a substantial Naval base'.

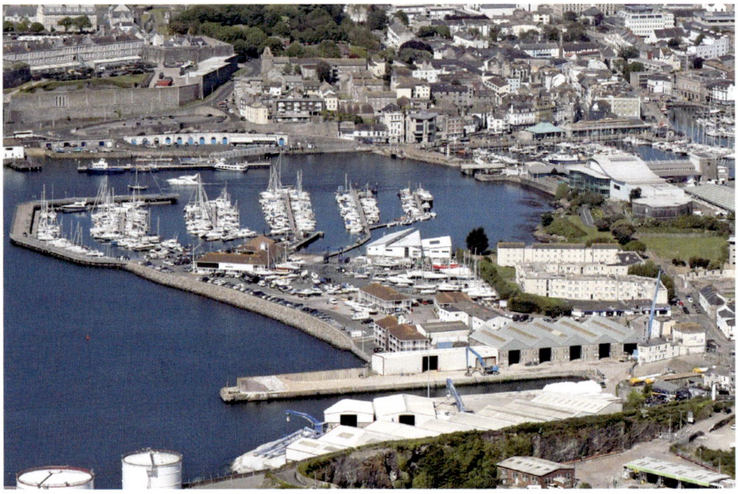

Site of Queen Anne's Battery.

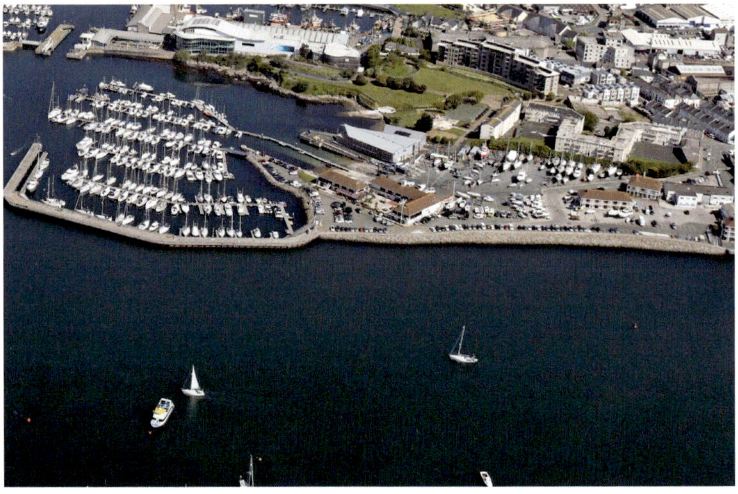

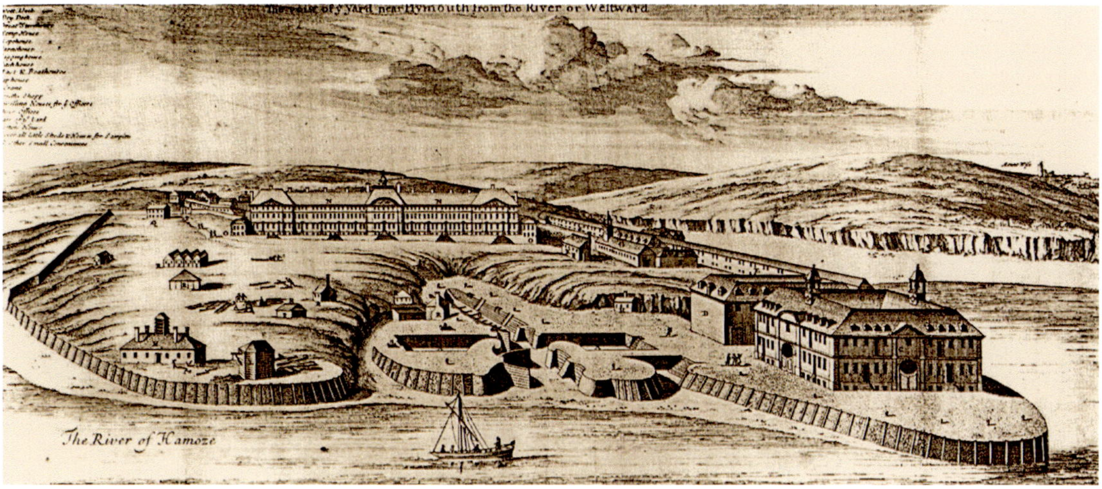

The dockyard, *c.* 1698. (Courtesy of the British Library Board, Lansdowne 847)

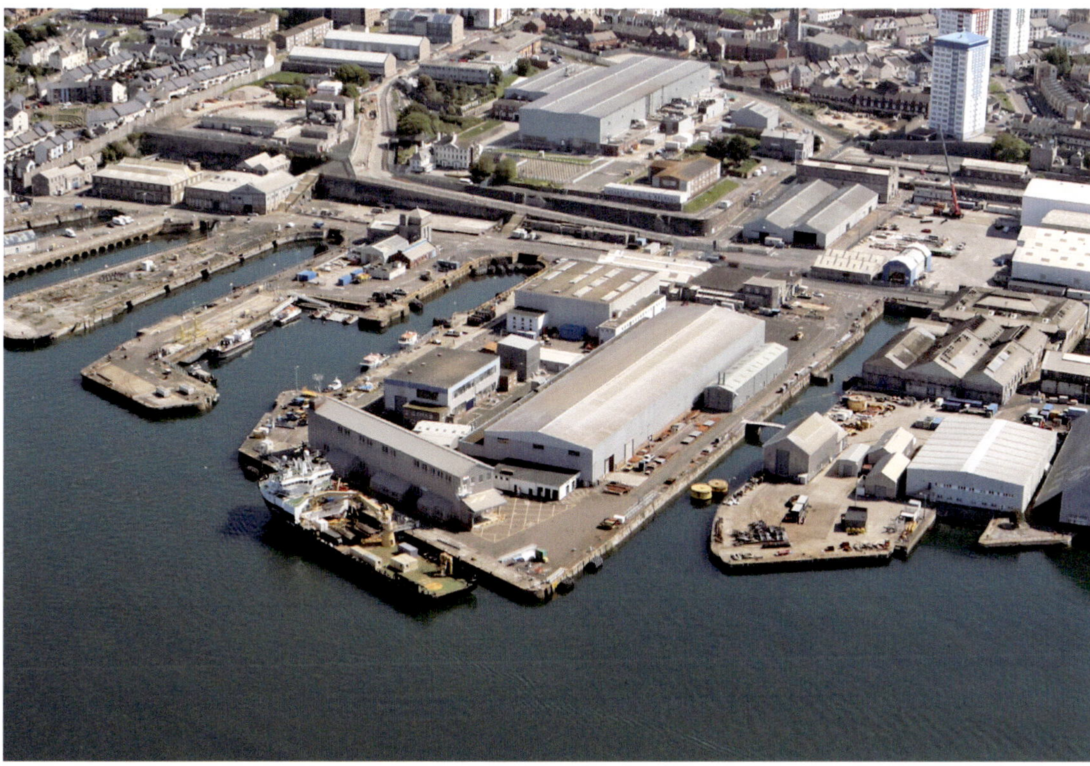

The original dockyard area today.

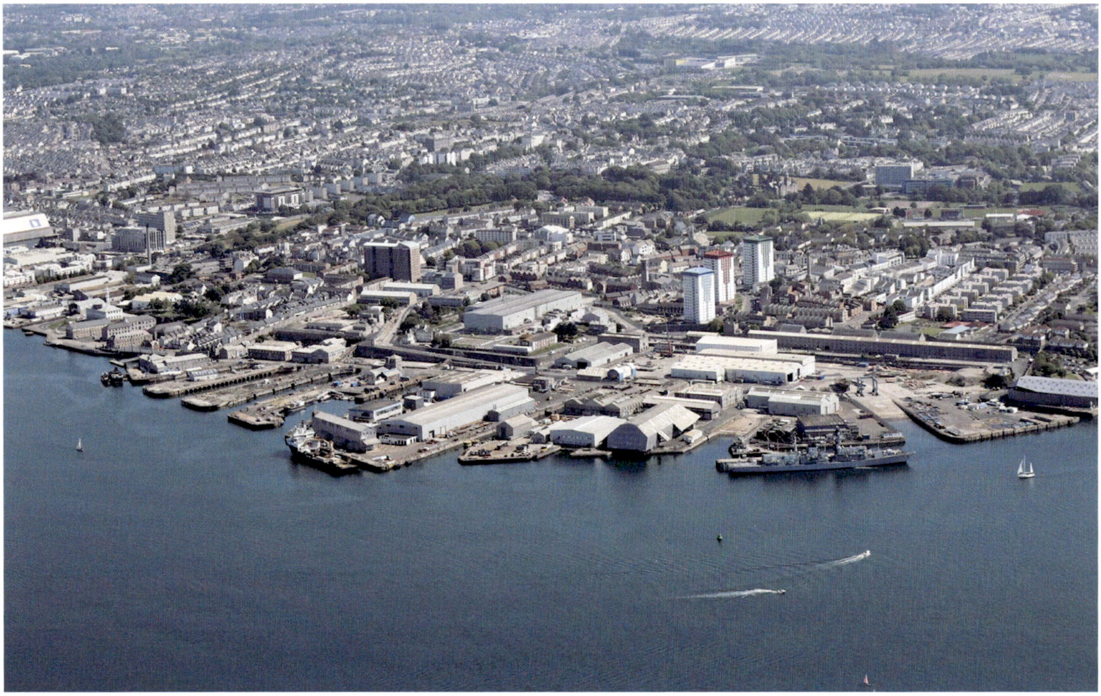

South Yard with the streets and houses of Devonport behind.

4. Eighteenth Century: The Hanoverians

England spent much of the eighteenth and early nineteenth centuries either at war or in immediate anticipation of it, which ensured continued expenditure on both the Royal Navy and coastal defence. In particular, local defences focused on protection of the channel into the Hamoaze and River Tamar, thus protecting the naval base that had been established there in the reign of William III (see previous chapter). Further defences were built in the late eighteenth century to protect the naval base from landward attacks, having been sanctioned by the Plymouth and Portsmouth Fortifications Act of 1758, which addressed this concern and allowed the construction of defences around what was then called Plymouth Dock.

In 1779 a joint Spanish and French fleet anchored in Cawsand Bay with the intention of landing troops and cannon to threaten the dockyard. This sharpened the minds of both politicians and senior soldiers. Amherst Battery, above the Cleave at Kingsand, which appears to have been built on the orders of Vice Admiral John Amherst when he was commanding Plymouth between 1776 and 1778, was possibly used to defend the bay during this time. Apparently, the invaders were forced out by the fortuitous combination of a storm and the timely arrival of a flotilla of Royal Navy ships under Sir Charles Hardy.

Following this threatened invasion, and given the improved cannon of the day, the government realised that a fleet could land soldiers at Cawsand Bay or even Whitsand Bay and haul cannon from there up on to Maker Heights. The cannon of this period were much improved from earlier ones: they were better made and designed to withstand much more pressure, so they were accurate at far greater ranges than in previous centuries. Firing from the top of Maker, they could have caused serious damage to Stonehouse, Plymouth and the dockyard. This provoked the building of a series of earthwork defence positions, including one above Cawsand and another at Picklecombe where those two forts were later built, plus the redoubts numbered 1 to 5 on top of Maker. No. 6 Redoubt, near Empacombe, was built slightly later, around 1803.

Devonport Lines

To protect it from land-based assaults, the naval dockyard was surrounded by 'the Dock Lines', initially consisting of stone and earthwork ramparts with large bastions – including the Marlborough Bastion to the north, Granby Bastion to the north-east, Stoke Bastion to the east and George Bastion to the south-east overlooking Stonehouse Pool – equipped with heavy guns and fronted by a shallow ditch, which stretched from the River Tamar north of the Gun Wharf in Morice Yard around to the Tamar, again below Mount Wise, effectively putting the whole town of Dock under military control.

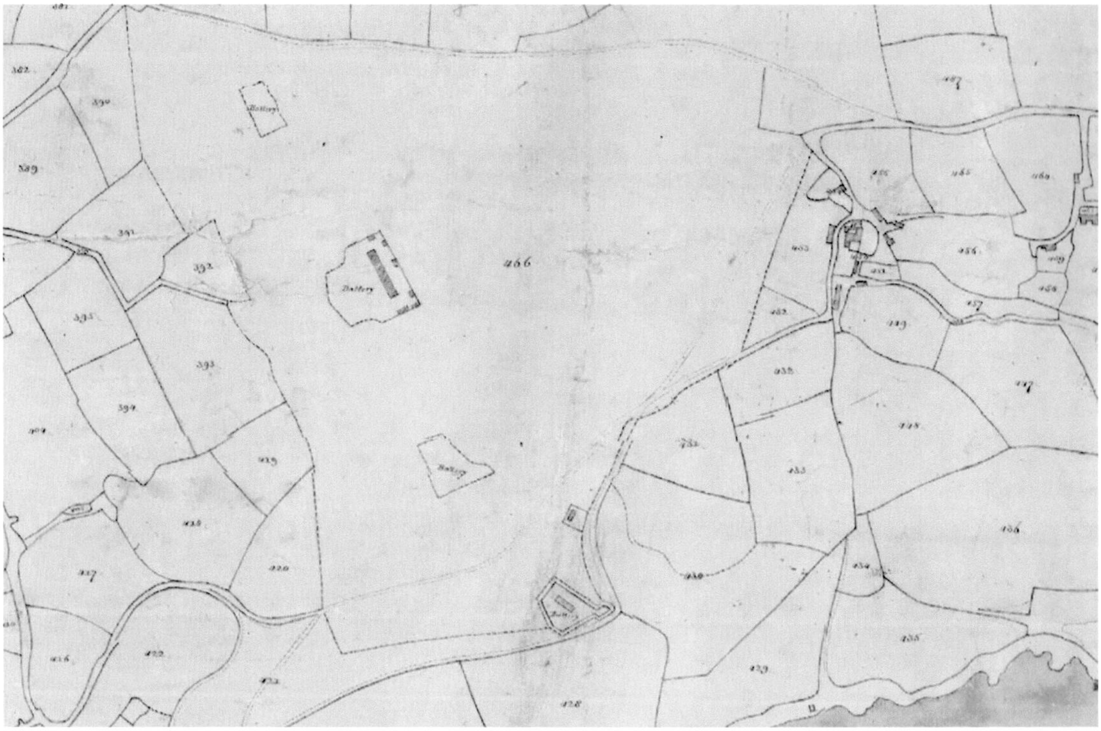

Maker tithe map showing Nos 1, 2, 3 and 4 redoubts.

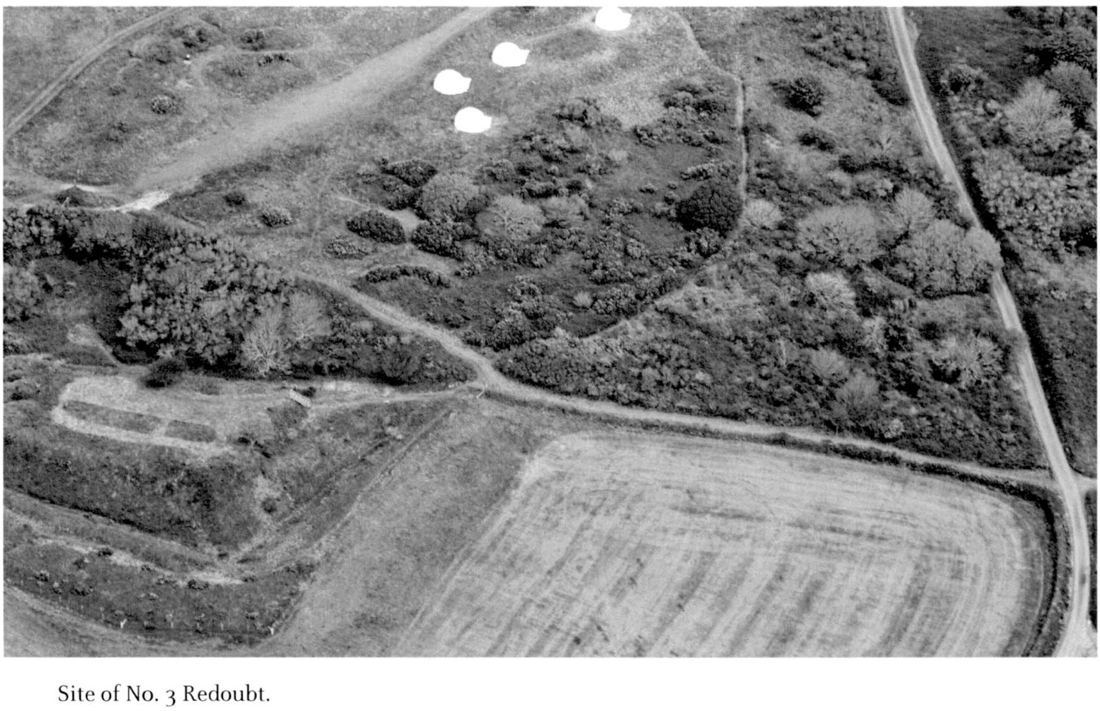

Site of No. 3 Redoubt.

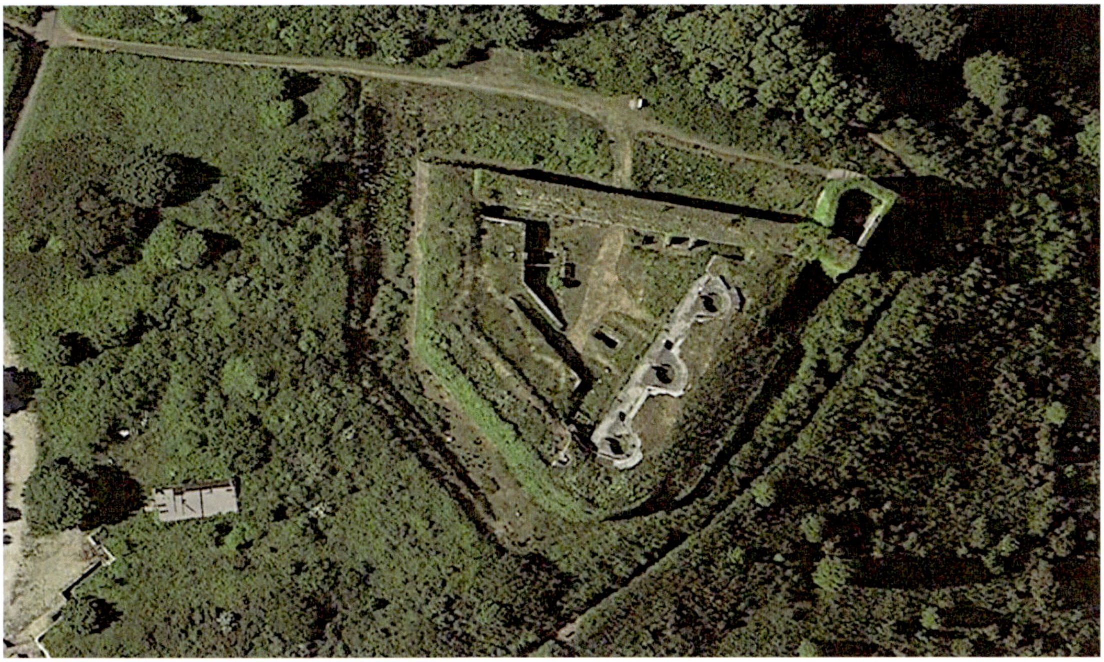

No. 4 Redoubt, later Grenville Battery.

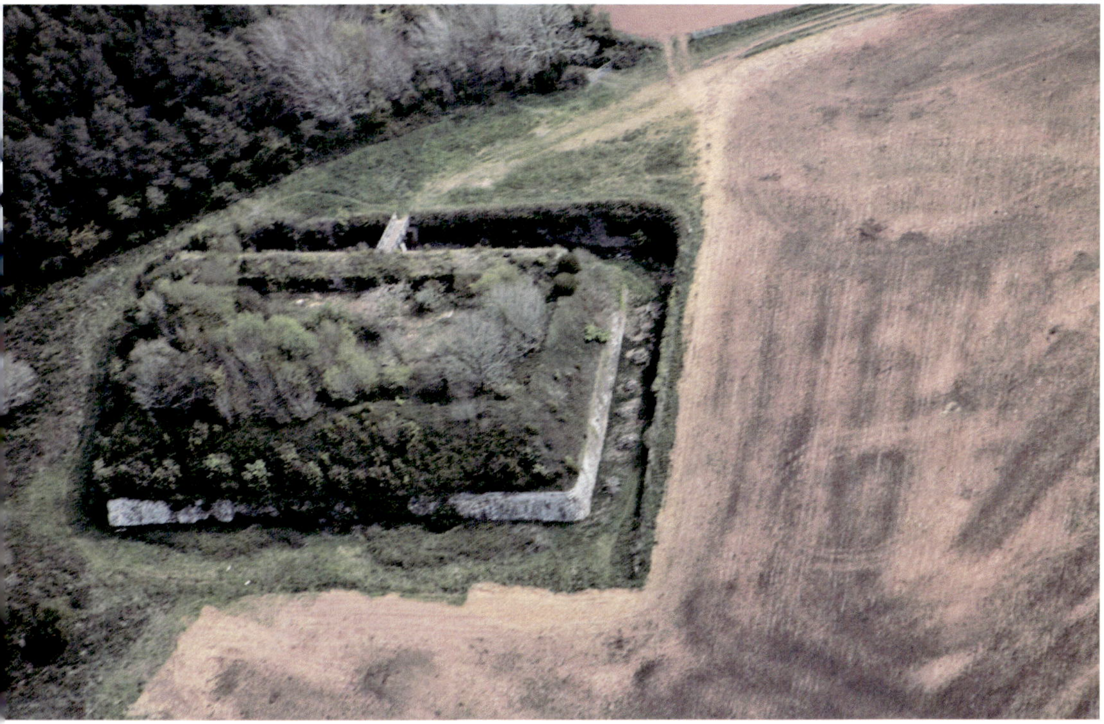

No. 5 Redoubt.

There were originally two gateways: the Stoke Barrier at the eastern end of Fore Street, giving access from Stoke, and the Stonehouse Barrier, guarding the hill approach from Stonehouse Creek at what is now called Devonport Hill. In the late 1780s the New Passage entrance was created, partly to improve access to a new Torpoint ferry crossing. These Lines were completed no later than 1765, although they were modified in the 1770s, 1780s and again in the early 1800s.

Sea access was controlled by batteries at Mount Wise and at Eastern and Western King overlooking Firestone Bay. These were built between 1779 and 1780, although they were significantly modified in later times, and a later battery was built in front of the old Western King Redoubt in the 1860s.

Various redoubts also helped protect the land approaches, including Mount Pleasant in Devonport, Stonehouse Battery and Bluff Battery beside Stonehouse Creek.

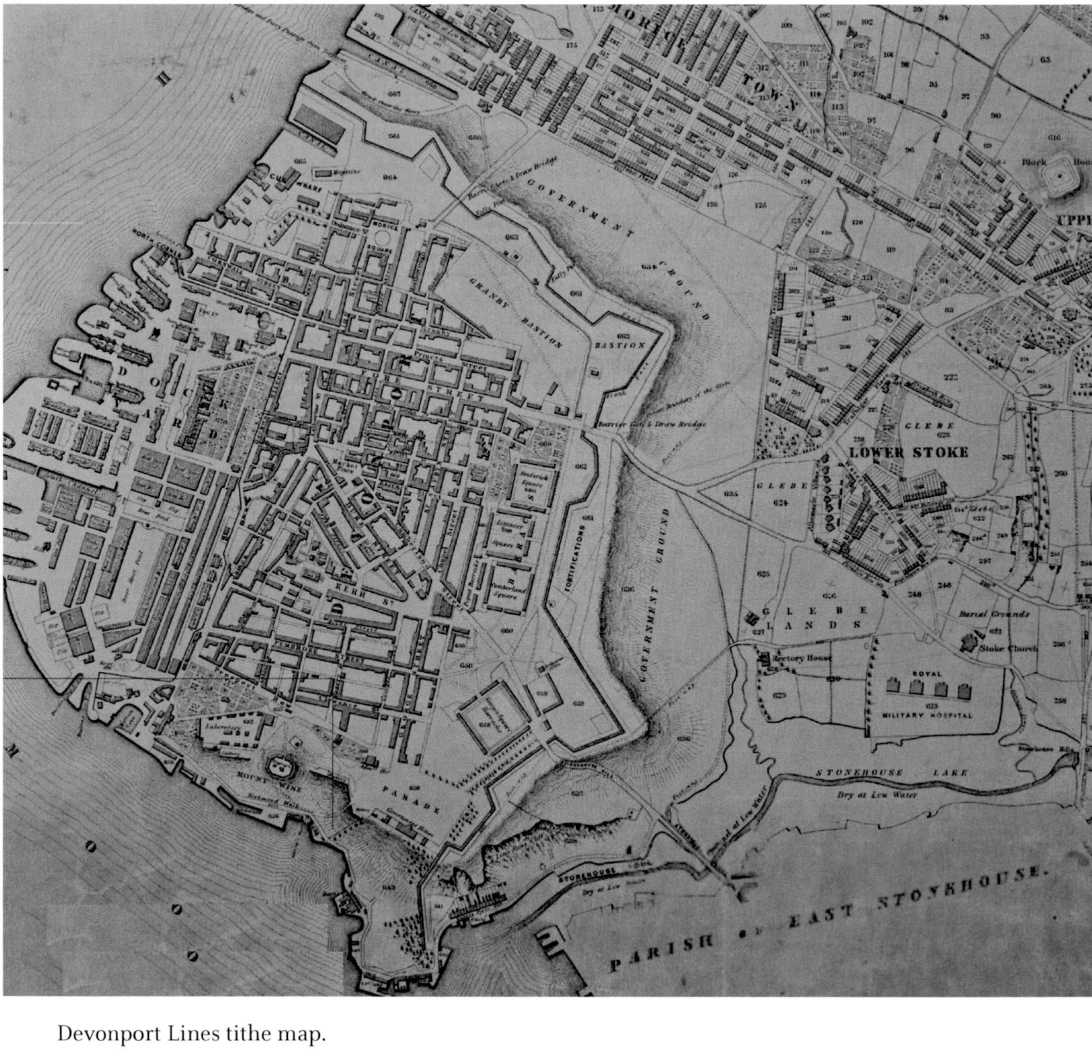

Devonport Lines tithe map.

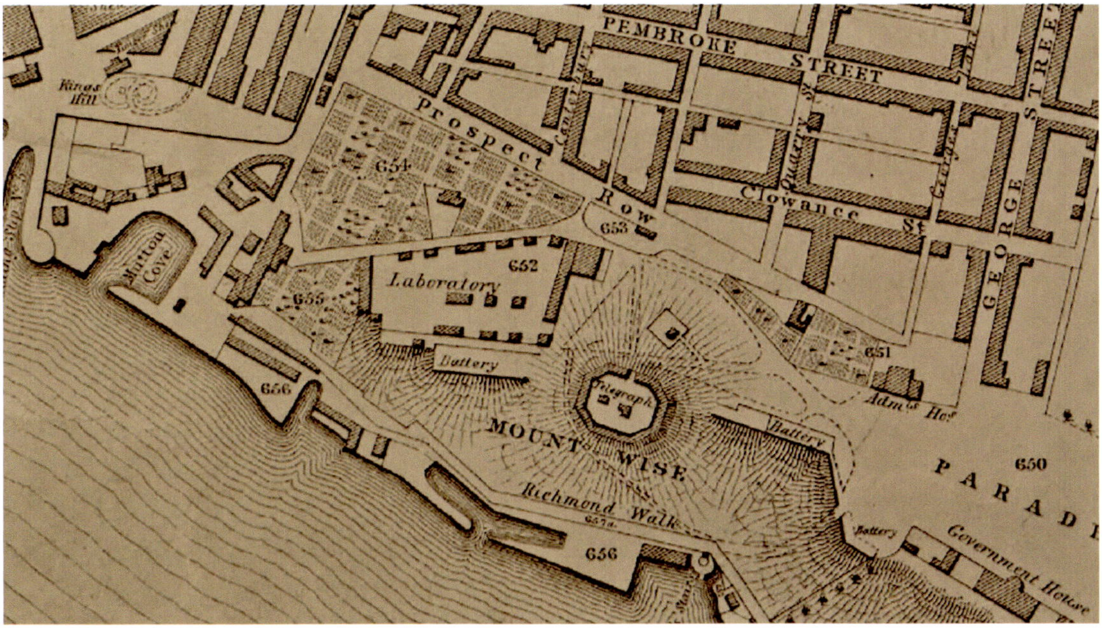

Mount Wise showing lab and batteries from tithe map.

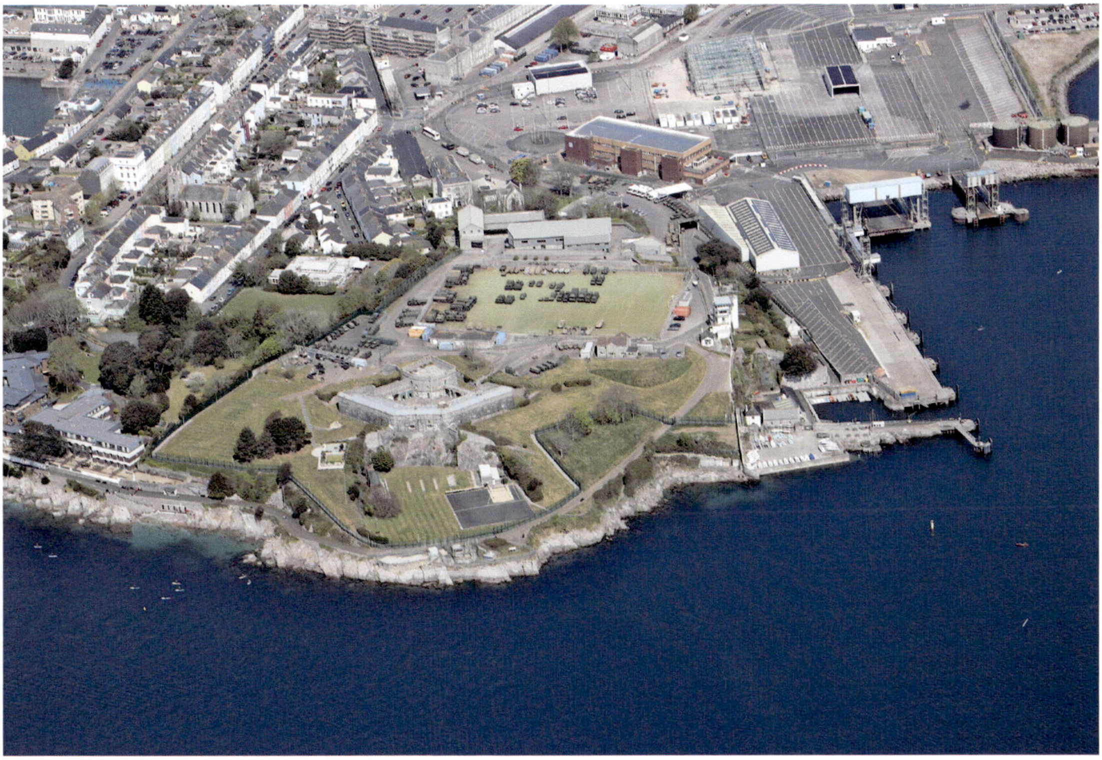

Eastern King.

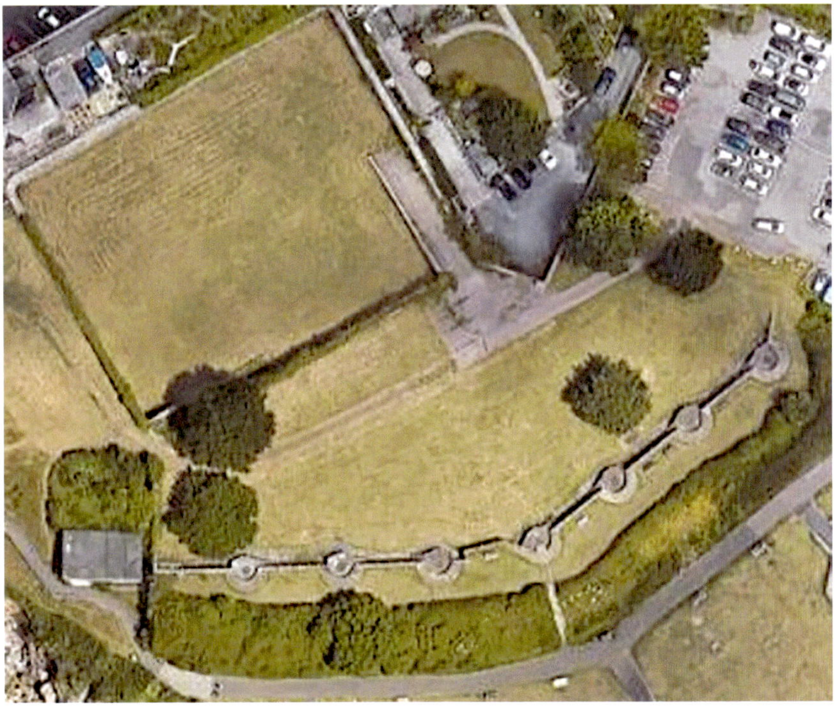

Western King.

The Devonport Blockhouse, or Mount Pleasant Redoubt, sits at the highest point of the park and was originally built in 1789. It was built to provide landward protection for the dockyard, which it overlooks, and to defend against an invading army because of tensions with America, France and Spain in the aftermath of the American Revolution.

The defences were upgraded in 1811 at the height of the Napoleonic Wars, but it was mothballed in 1815 when the war with France ended and was not recommissioned. When the blockhouse was destroyed by fire in 1855 it was not rebuilt.

In the Second World War the site housed anti-aircraft guns and a barrage balloon to defend Devonport Dockyard and was also used by ARP wardens due to its far-reaching views across the city.

After the war the remains of the Blockhouse were demolished, leaving just the foundations and earthworks, and the site opened as a public park. There is a play area, a community centre and numerous paths to make the best of the stunning view.

Within the square formed by the modern Millbay Road, Hobart Street, East Street, and the part of Stonehouse Street that joins Millbay Road, there used to be a hill, commonly known as Stonehouse Hill or Battery Hill after the defensive battery that was built on top of it.

Bluff Battery was also built at this time, on top of a hill beside the later Stonehouse Bridge.

The fortifications on Drake's Island were upgraded as well. They were built between 1779 and 1780 on the orders of Colonel Dixon to counter the threat posed by a Franco-Spanish fleet anchored in Cawsand Bay as previously mentioned.

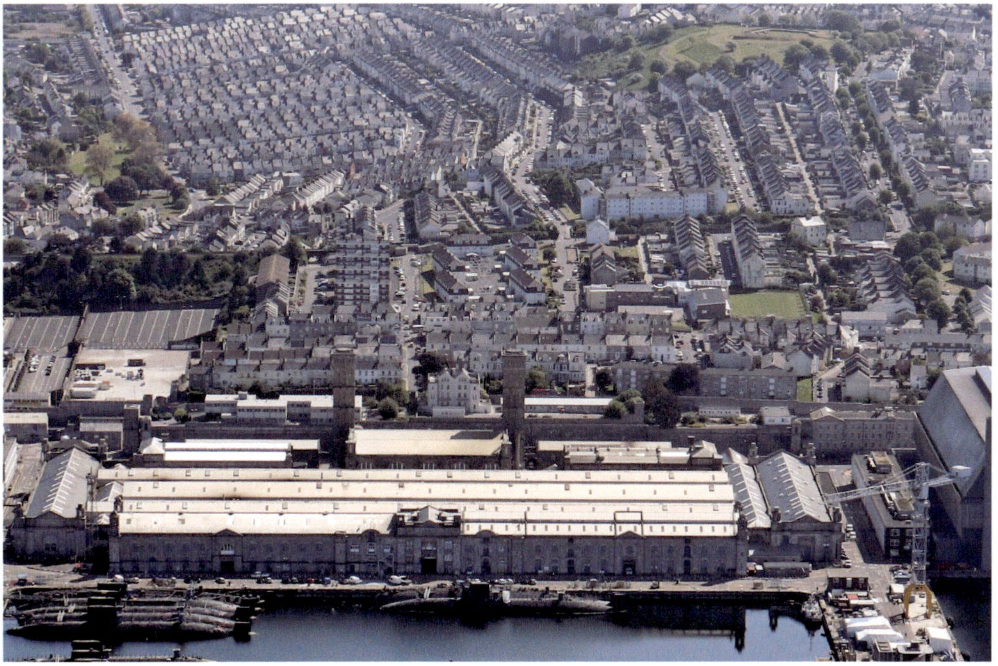

Blockhouse Park, site of Mount Pleasant Redoubt, seen to the top right on the hill overlooking the dockyard.

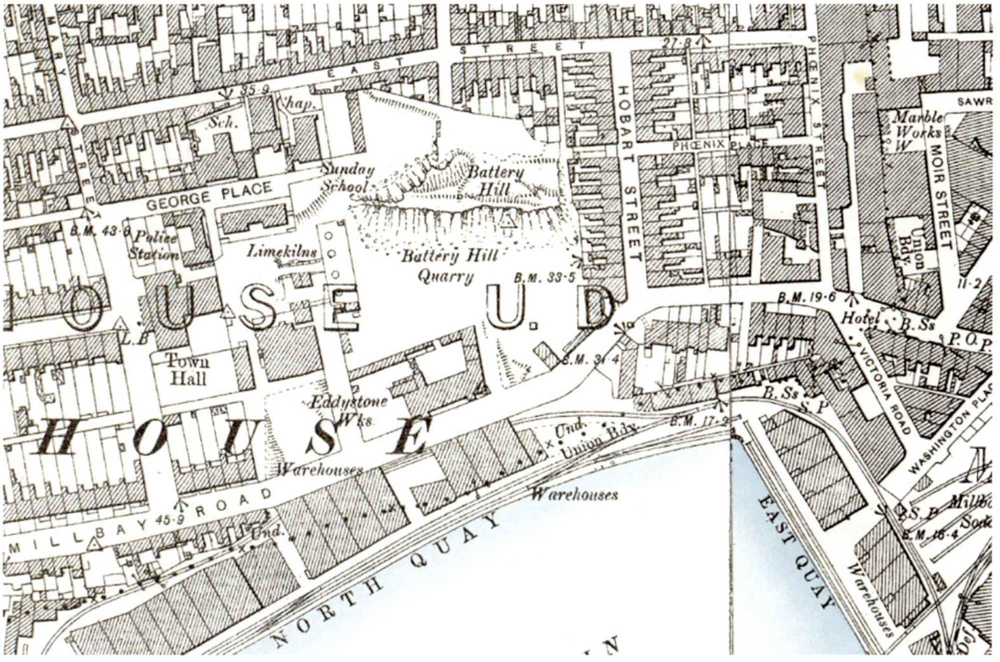

Site of Stonehouse Battery on an OS map. (Reproduced with the permission of the National Library of Scotland, CC-BY 4.0)

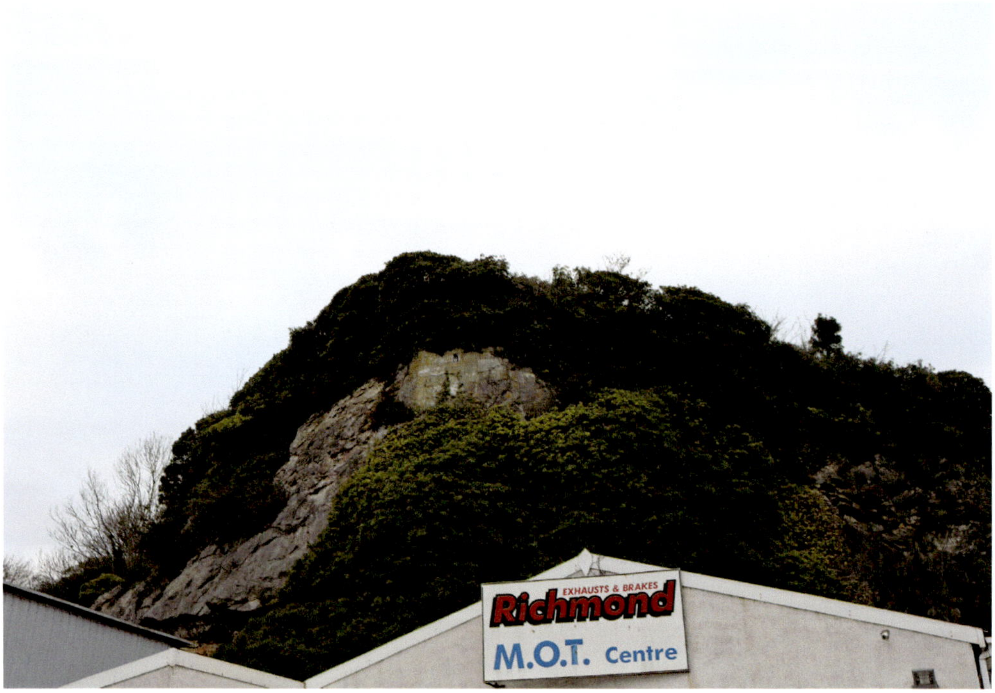

Bluff Battery.

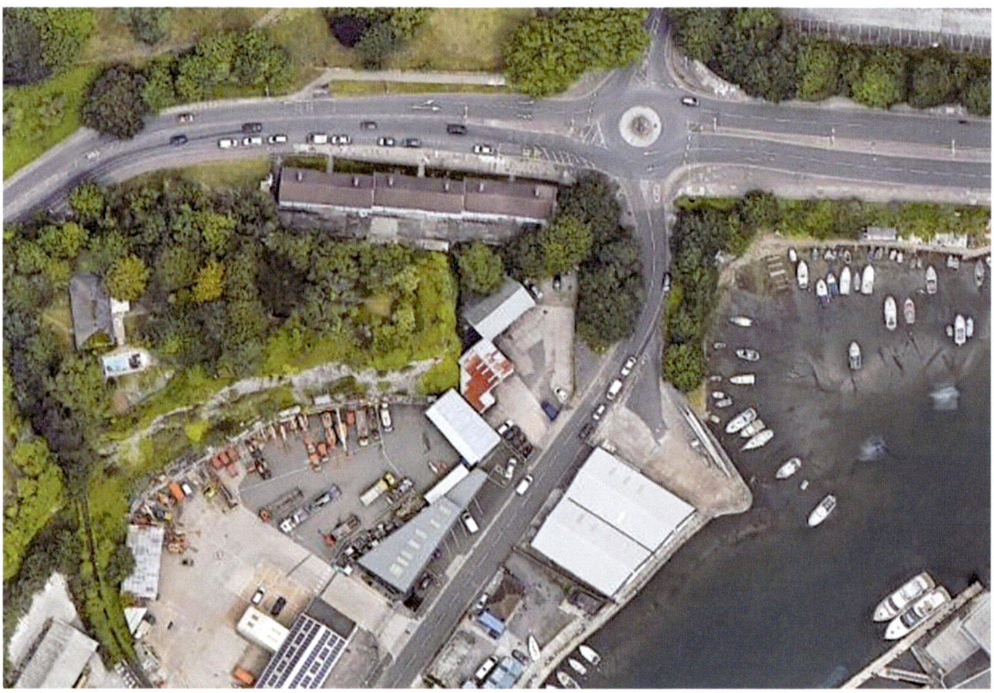

Site of Bluff Battery beside Devonport Hill.

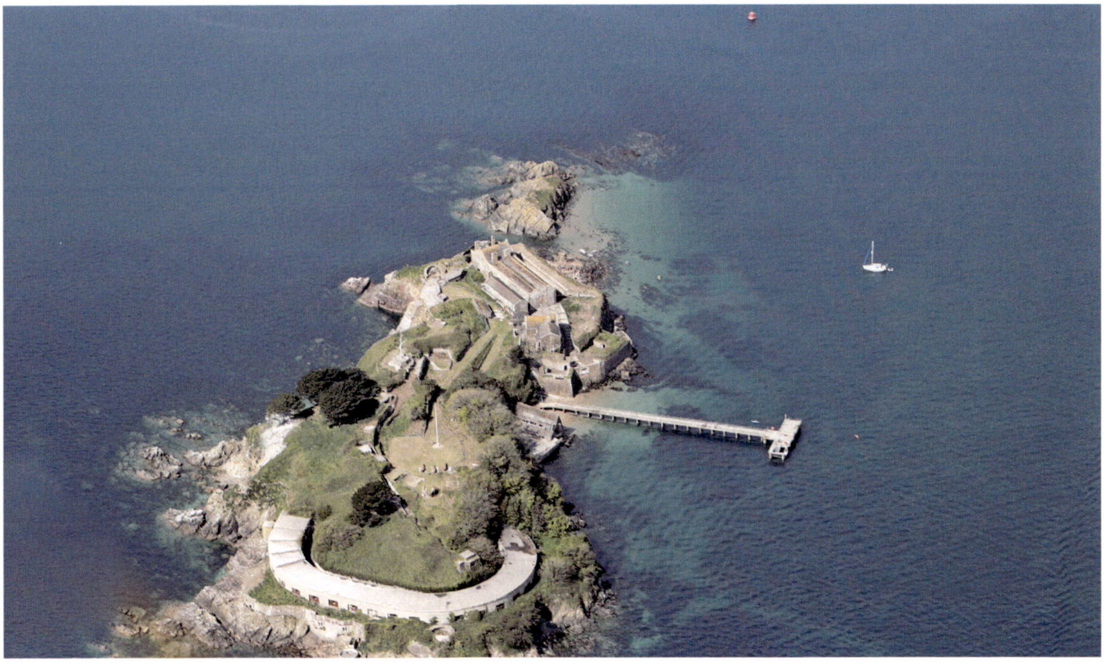

Drake's Island.

Dock Lines

In 1787 the Lines were further fortified by the addition of six barracks or squares – Marlborough, Granby, Frederick, Ligonier, Cumberland and George squares. They were surrounded by a wall, known as the King's Interior Boundary Wall, with fortifications and large entrances described on the tithe map of 1841 as 'Barrier Gate with drawbridge'. It's amazing to think now that at that time anyone entering or leaving Devonport from Plymouth had to do so via a defended arch at Stonehouse Hill; those entering via Fore Street, or what we now call Marlborough Street, had to do so via a drawbridge! The gate barriers and the barracks were all linked by a military road. Outside of the Lines, the War Department also owned the fields to the north and east of the town. These were cleared of all trees and hedges and kept free of any later building development, forming a glacis – an open area providing no cover for the enemy. The site is now effectively that of Devonport Park and Brickfields.

Although the Duke of Wellington condemned the fortifications as being inadequate in 1815, the work continued until 1853. However, as the science of warfare developed, the Lines became redundant. Between 1854 and 1858 the old squares were demolished and replaced with Raglan Barracks. The drawbridges were removed in 1865 and the archway on Devonport Hill was removed in 1877. Finally, the trenches were filled in during 1886, although a 25-inch-to-the-mile OS map of 1892 showed one section of trench remaining, running from New Passage Hill beside the old Royal Albert Hospital, now a housing estate with some industrial units.

Since the end of the Second World War most of the Lines and barracks have been swept away, with only isolated remnants that have listed building status, such as the Raglan Barracks Gatehouse, left to testify to Devonport's great military past.

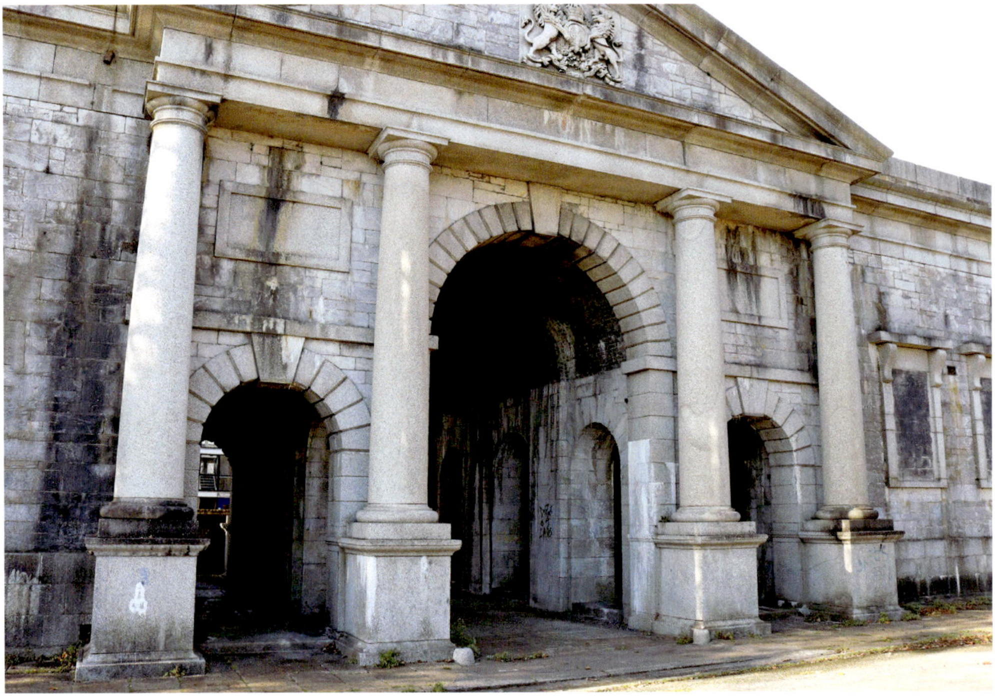

Raglan Barracks entrance.

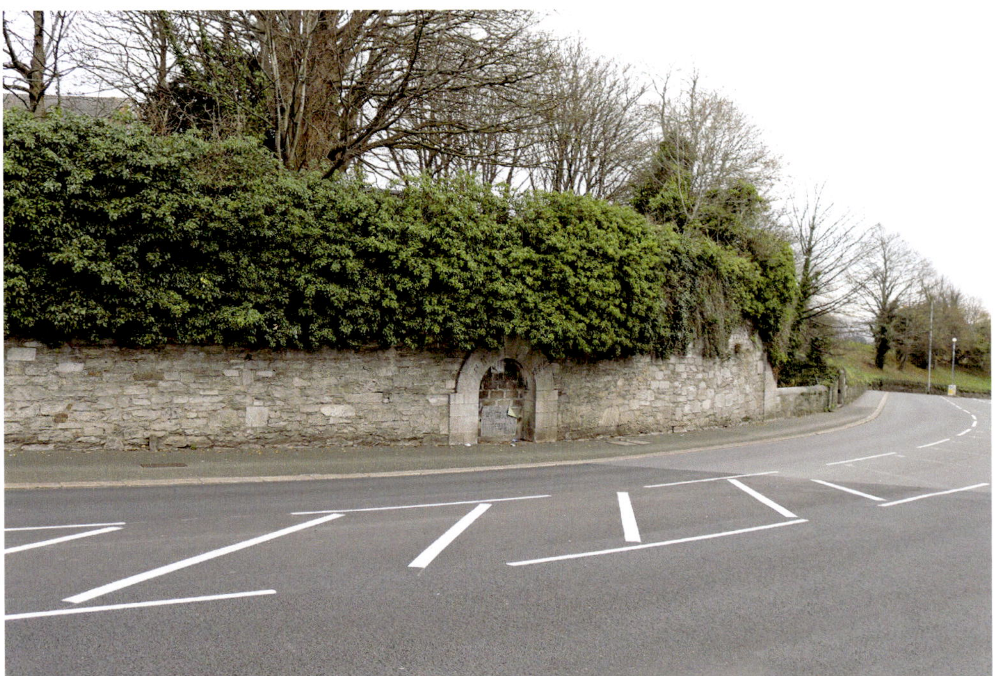

Remaining traces of the Devonport Lines.

Staddon Battery

As previously mentioned, in Henry VIII's time a battery was constructed on the cliffs overlooking the Sound. This was called Staddon Battery, and it was rebuilt in 1779 into a ten-gun battery with a square guardhouse to its rear. When paired with the redoubts on Maker Heights, it offered coverage across the expanse of Plymouth Sound. It has been demolished and is now the site of Staddon Cottage.

Also built in this era was Stonehouse Barracks. The Royal Marine Corps had been formed in 1664 and Marines had previously been billeted around Plymouth and Dock, but there was a growing need for a permanent base for them. Following the building of Stonehouse Bridge in 1767 access to Royal Navy ships at Dock was much improved, so Stonehouse was an ideal place for such a base. Lord Mount Edgcumbe owned all of Stonehouse, so he sold the government some land adjoining Millbay, which was an ideal site with access to the sea. Work started in 1781, with the first Marines moving in during 1783. The site provided an almost self-contained barracks, with three accommodation blocks surrounding the parade ground. This was initially separated from the public by railings, although later in 1867 the old Barrack Street was demolished and the new west block added, forming the impressive entrance we know today fronting onto Durnford Street.

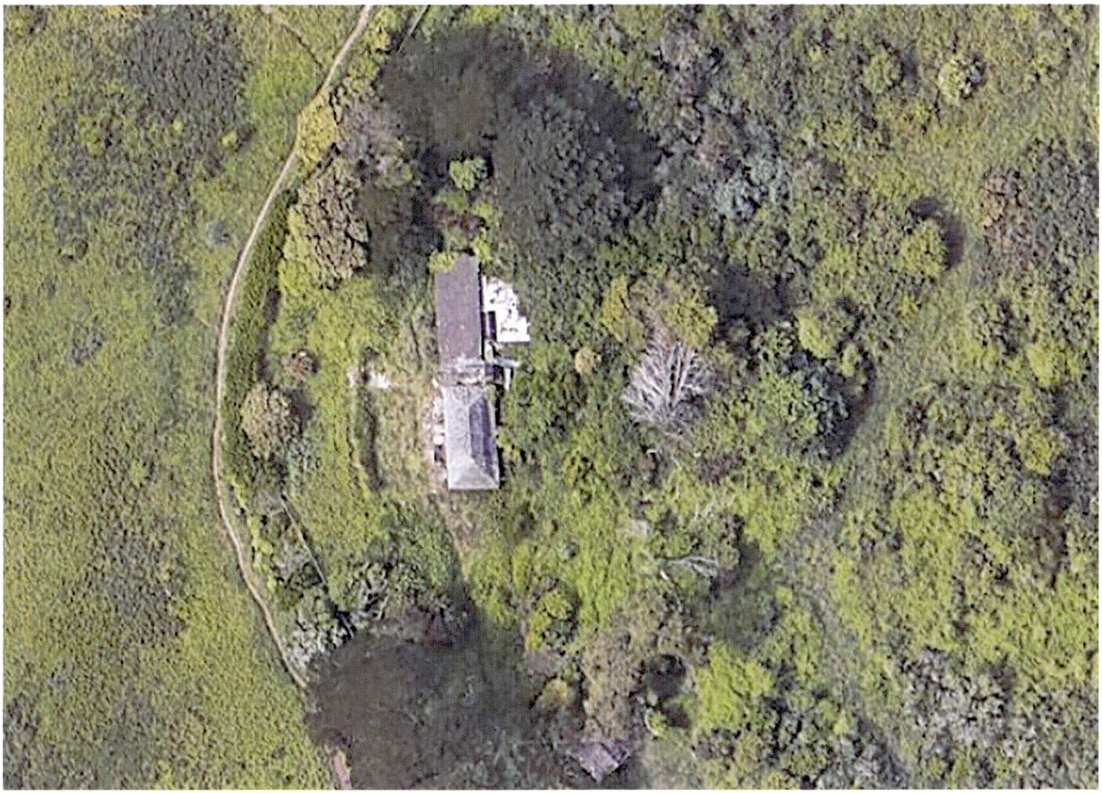

Staddon Heights Battery site.

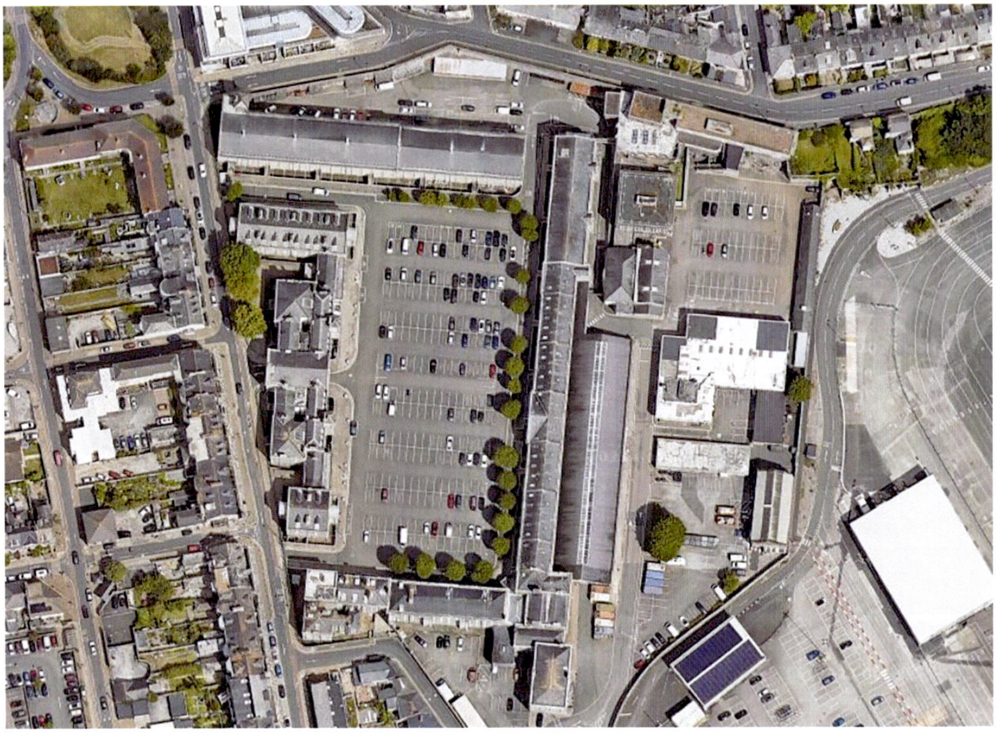

Royal Marines barracks.

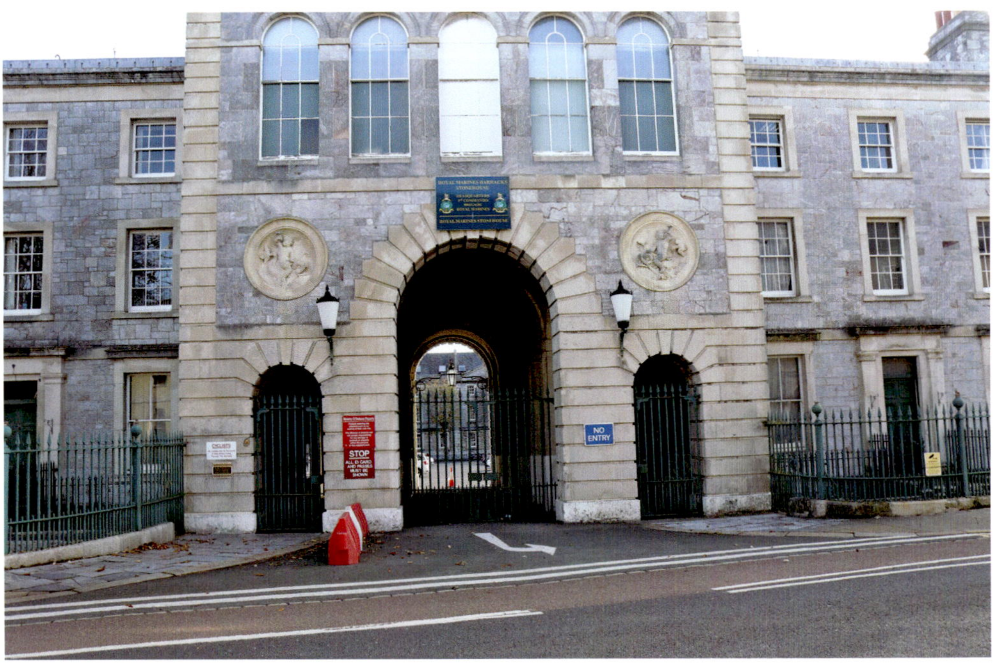

Stonehouse Barracks gatehouse.

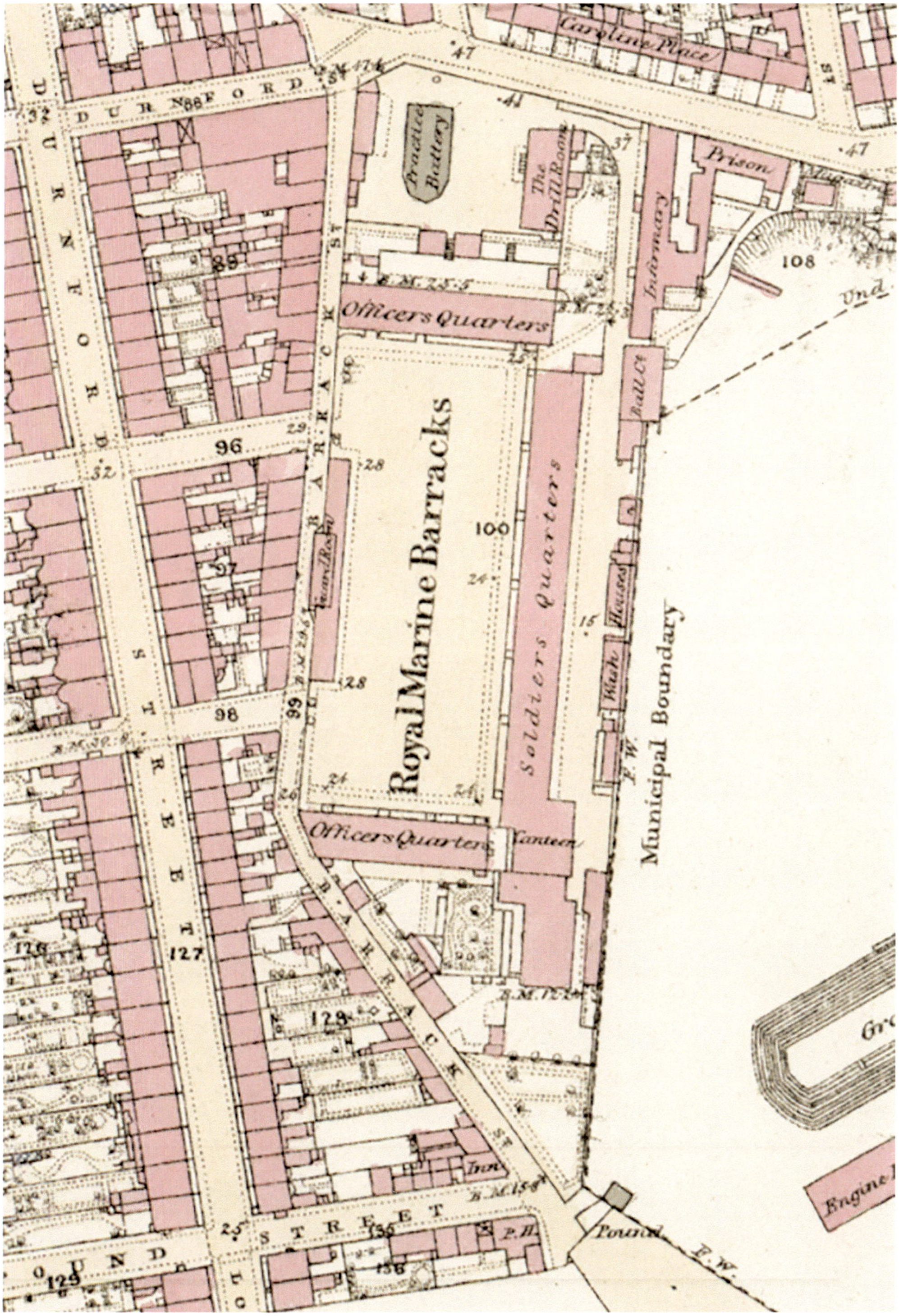

Stonehouse Barracks on an 1866 OS map. (Reproduced with the permission of the National Library of Scotland, CC-BY 4.0)

5. Nineteenth Century: Victoria

The nineteenth century was a time of enormous expenditure on defences of all kinds, against both sea- and land-based attack.

1800–25

One of the earliest structures built at this time was Maker Barracks, which was constructed in 1804–08 on the site of the old No. 2 Redoubt. The barrack was built to accommodate the soldiers needed to man the other late eighteenth-century redoubts on Maker Heights. The barracks first appear in the census of 1851 when there were thirty people living there, including wives and children, from eight families. Now used for community purposes, it is a Grade II* listed building.

The early years of the century saw a laboratory built at Mount Wise, as shown on a plan dated 1811. Built for the Board of Ordnance, it comprised a collection of widely

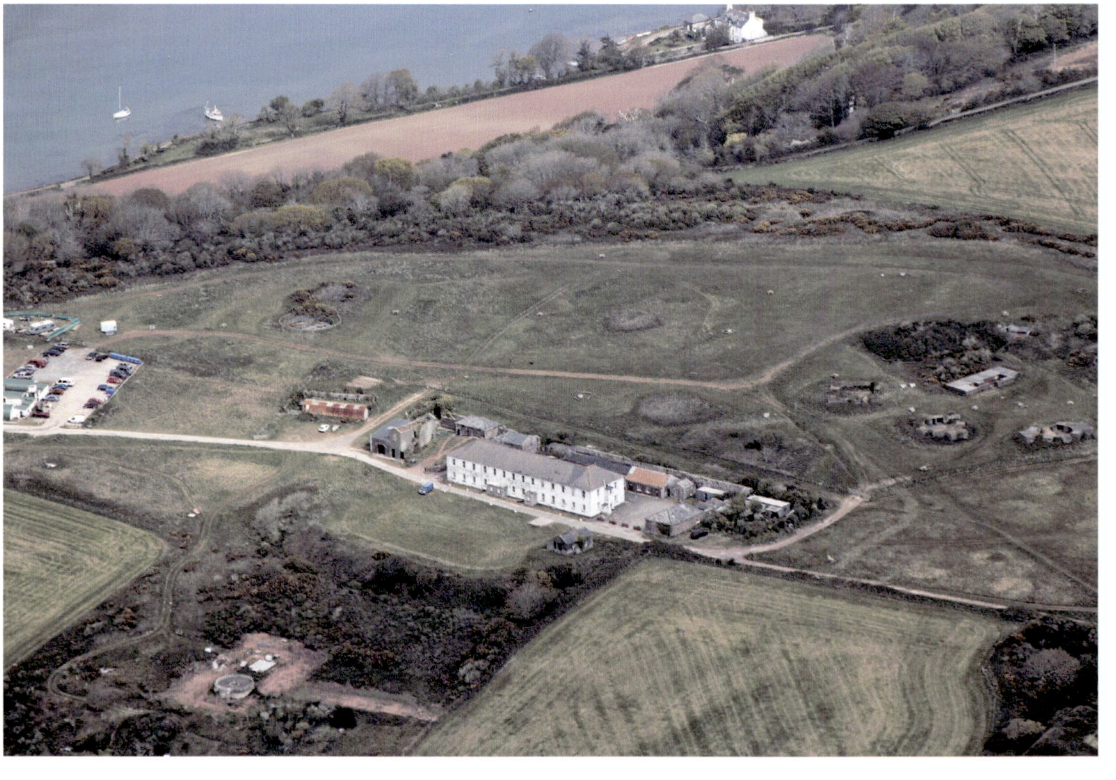

Maker Barracks, site of No. 2 Redoubt.

spaced buildings for the refurbishing and testing of explosive devices for the use of the Royal Navy. It was situated at the very southern end of Plymouth Dock between Mutton Cove and Mount Wise. It only stayed in operation as a laboratory for twenty years or so; by 1834 it was converted for use as barracks and remained in military use well into the twentieth century. Given the number of military establishments around, barracks to house all the soldiers were very necessary.

According to Brian Mosely's excellent Old Devonport website, it was described thus in 1823:

> The Laboratory consist of twenty-one detached buildings, inclosed [*sic*] by a high wall, and forming an oblong square (?). These buildings are designed to be used as workshops, for smiths, joiners, harness makers, and other tradesmen employed in the manufactory of stores requisite for an equipment of a military expedition. Neat houses for officers are erected on the eastern side, where the entrance is also situated.

The site is now part of a housing development called Garrison Close, which appears to have been built within the original walls, just to the west of the Mount Wise Observation Tower.

Another large barracks was built at Millbay. Again, to quote Brian Mosely, this time from his Old Plymouth website:

> A description of the Barracks from 'The Picture of Plymouth', published in 1812, reads:
>
> 'Temporary barracks have been erected here capable of holding 1,000 men; apartments for the officers are stationed near them. The first enclosure contains the guard-room for

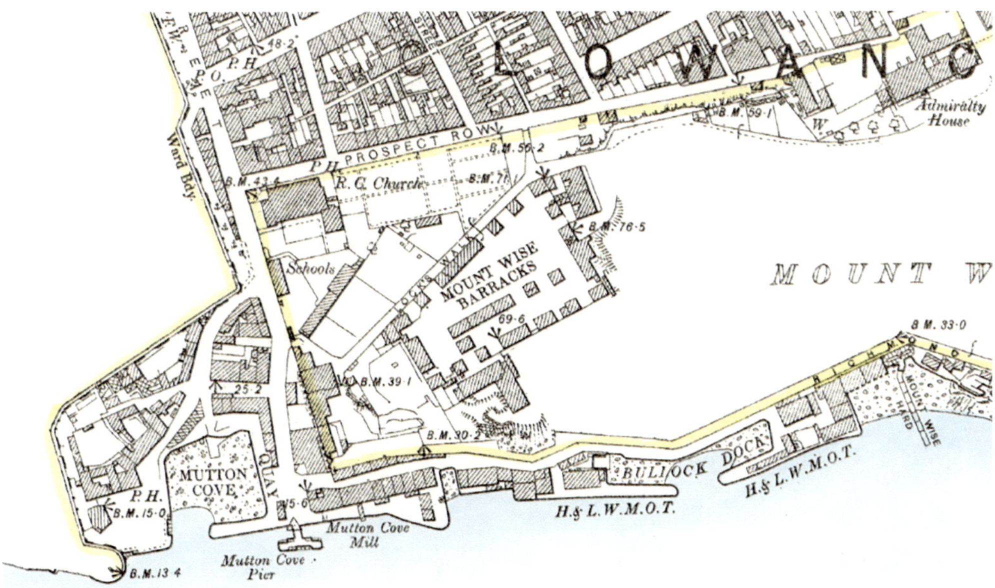

Mount Wise Barracks on an 1895 OS map. (Reproduced with the permission of the National Library of Scotland, CC-BY 4.0)

the prison, where a captain's guard is daily mounted, and various necessary appendages to the barracks are placed; in the second enclosure are the barracks and a hospital for the sick. The prospect from this parade is a very fine one. At present the Shropshire Militia are quartered here.'

The barracks was built on the site of what had been the Millbay Prison for prisoners of war. The site the barracks occupied is now a grassy slope and sports field in Millbay Park, behind the Duke of Cornwall Hotel. The old drill ground is now home to the Devon Army Cadet Force centre.

The high ground at Staddon, with its excellent views over the Sound, reflected those of Maker. Five redoubts had been built on Maker in the eighteenth century (see previous chapter). At that time a Tudor redoubt on Staddon Heights had been rebuilt as a 'ten gun battery with a square guardhouse to its rear'. The effectiveness of these batteries was improved immensely when, between 1811 and 1848, the Breakwater was built. Ships coming into the Sound were forced to go either side of it, thus bringing them nearer to one or other of the batteries.

This increased the Staddon Heights Battery's importance, prompting it to be rebuilt again in 1811, with further magazines added and an enlarged guardhouse. It remained in use as a coastal defence battery until 1853 when it was replaced by Staddon Point Battery (still there, above and behind the later Fort Bovisand). The original Heights Battery has been demolished and is now the site of Staddon Cottage.

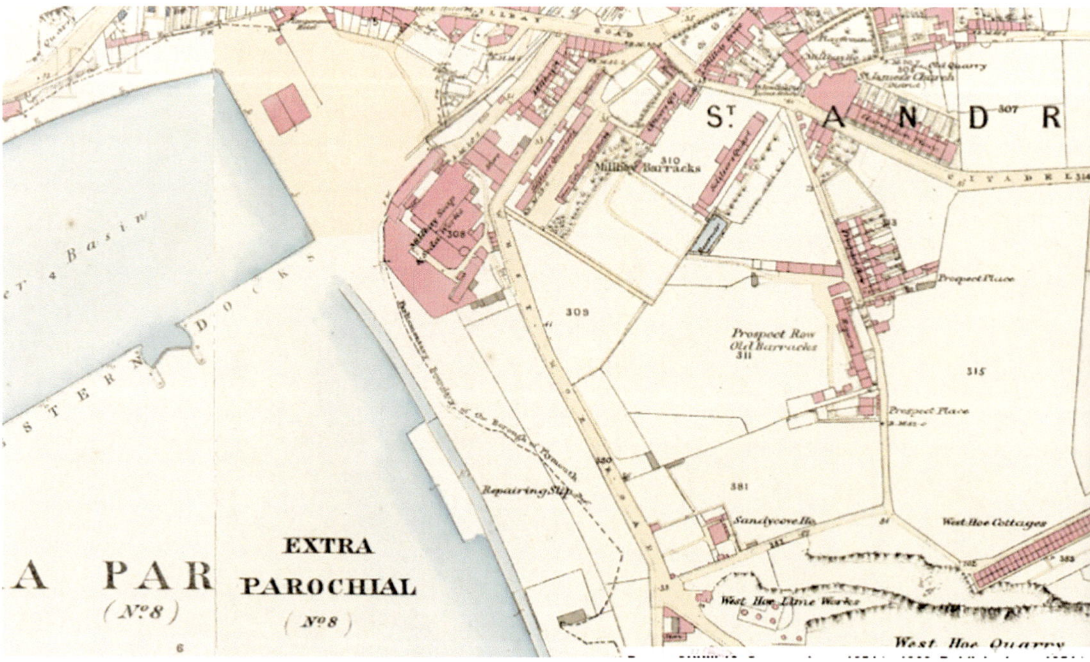

Millbay Barracks on an 1895 OS map. (Reproduced with the permission of the National Library of Scotland, CC-BY 4.0)

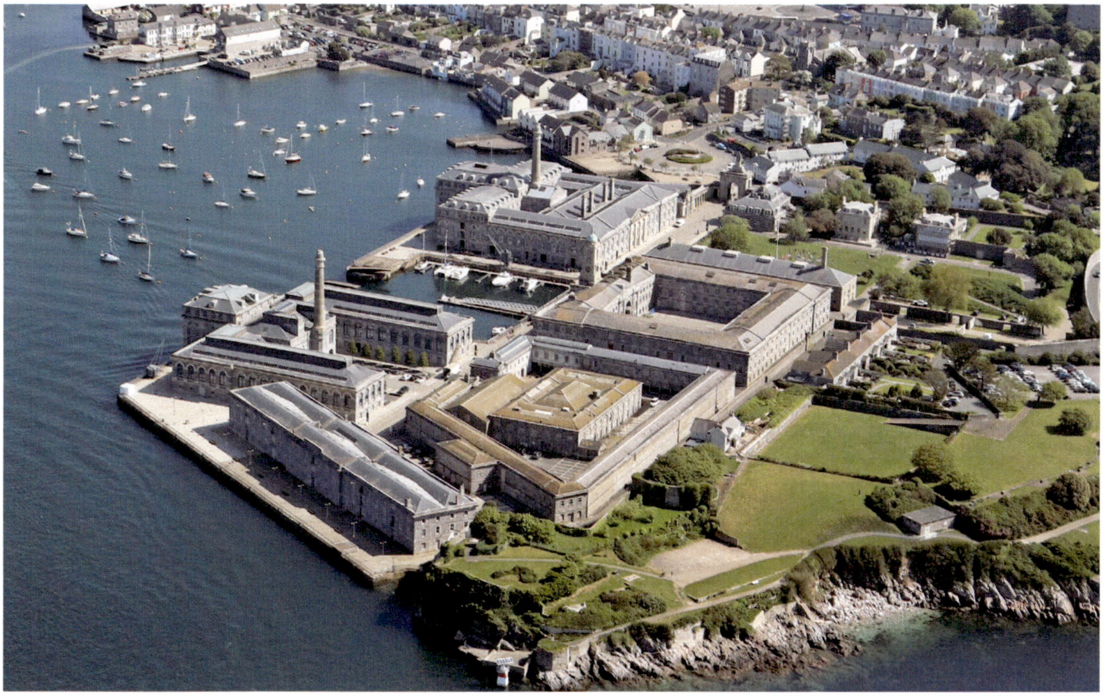

Royal William Yard.

Royal William Victualling Yard, named after King William IV, was not exactly a part of Plymouth's defences, but was still very important to the Royal Navy. It was built between 1824 and 1835 to replace the seventeenth-century victualling stores on Lambhay Hill and centralise the other places scattered around the Plymouth area, including the King's Brewhouse and the gunpowder works at Southdown, Millbrook, which between them had produced everything required by naval ships. It also provided space for administration, accommodation and large amounts of storage.

An 1824 Act of Parliament sanctioned the purchase of the site from the Earl of Mount Edgcumbe and John Renney was appointed as architect. It took two years to level the site and in 1827 work began on the first of the buildings. The yard remained in operation until 1992.

1825–50

Again, though not originally built as part of Plymouth's defences, the Emigration Depot in Plymouth was constructed in 1847 on the quayside overlooking Sutton Harbour. This was where desperate people came to take up the assisted passages available to Australia and Canada. Over the nearly fifty years it was operating, many thousands of Brits left for new lives in these countries – up to 1,800 emigrants in a single week.

By 1893 financial problems in both Canada and Australia brought an end to assisted passages, and by 1897 the depot became Elphinstone Barracks and thus part of the defences. Now long gone, its site is now Elphinstone car park.

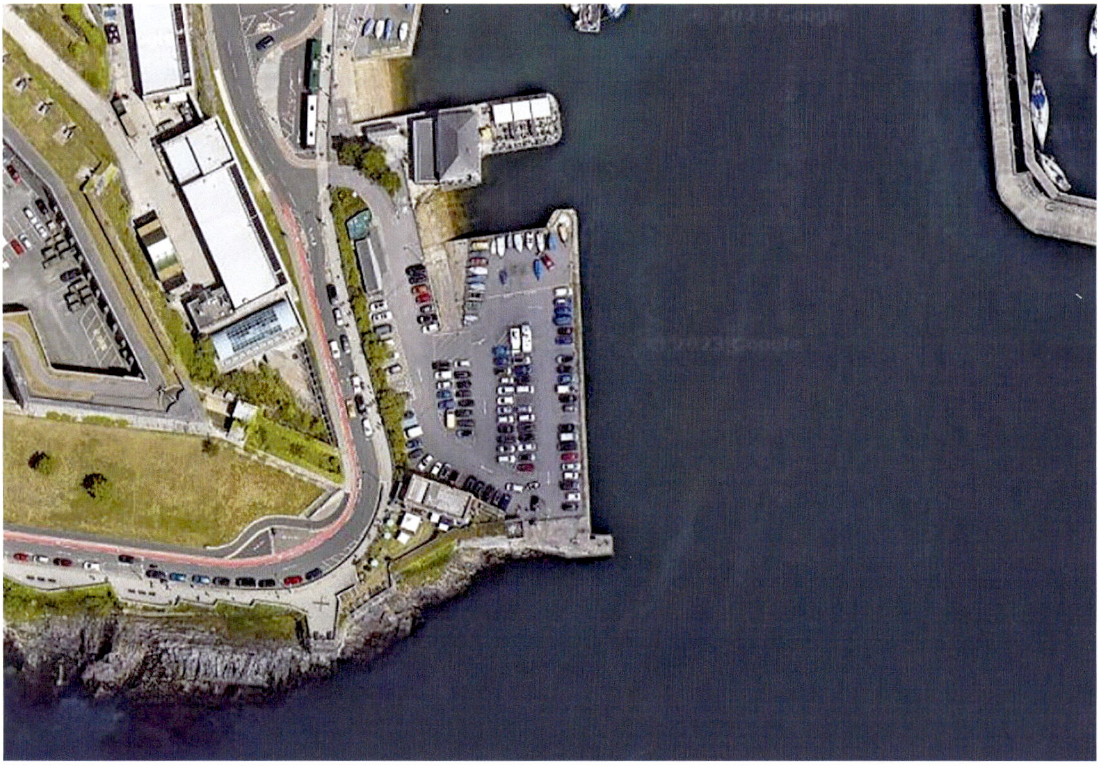

Site of Elphinstone Barracks.

Whilst some expenditure had been made on coastal defence, including construction of the new Eastern King Battery, renamed Prince of Wales Redoubt, and the defensible barracks on the site of the previous earthwork at Picklecombe between 1844 and 1849, on the whole the defences around the country had been neglected in favour of maintaining an enhanced naval fleet. Britain's defence policy relied upon the Royal Navy to protect both the homeland and the increasing number of colonies and possessions overseas. To ensure domination, the Royal Navy was maintained at a strength greater than the combined size of its two biggest competitors.

1850–75

From the 1860s and into the twentieth century the Royal Dockyard was expanded to the north into the Keyham area to cope with new technology, forming what became known as the Steam Yard.

Bull Point Royal Artillery Barracks was built between 1851 and 1855 to house the officers and soldiers of the Royal Artillery, guarding the extremely important Bull Point Ordnance Depot, north of the dockyard, and to help protect the new area of the Royal Dockyard from any possible enemy invasion from the north. It also was a defensible barracks, rather than a fort. It contained quarters for soldiers and officers, a parade ground and magazine.

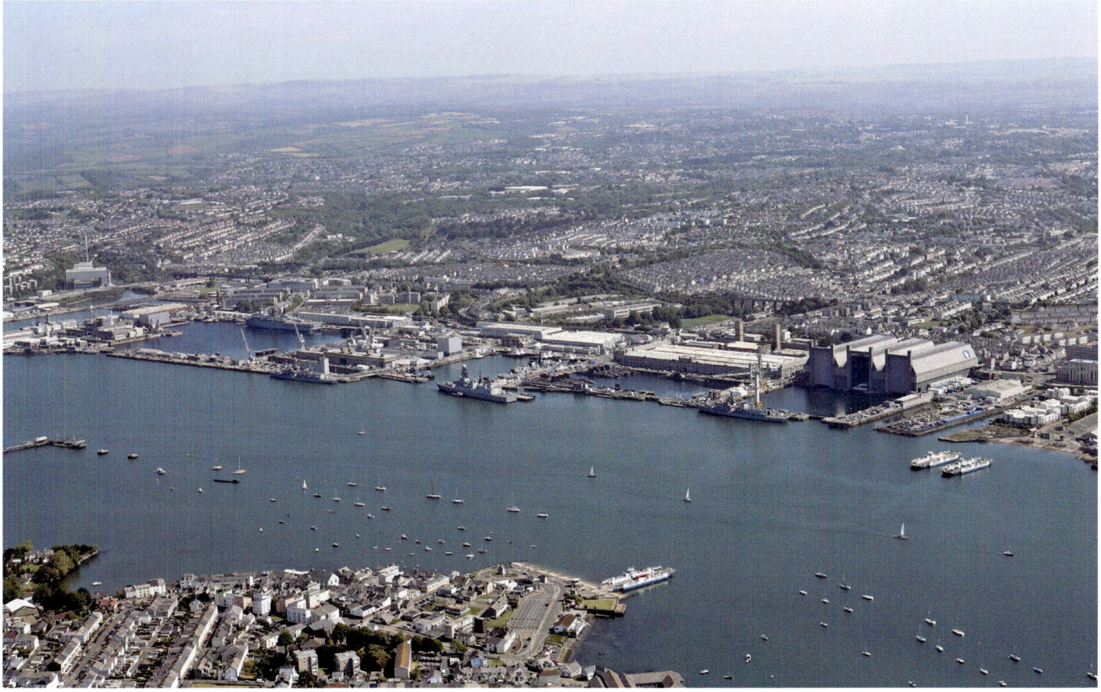

The Steam Yard or North Yard.

Bull Point Royal Artillery Barracks still exists alongside Foulston Avenue, St Budeaux, and is Grade II listed.

Now we reach the time when things became very expensive! In December 1851 Louis-Napoleon, President of France, declared himself Emperor Napoleon III. Despite British concerns, tensions were eased when the two countries worked together during the Crimean War (1853–56) where they allied to fight against Russia. Then, in 1858 the French launched the world's first seagoing ironclad warship, *La Gloire*, starting an arms race with Britain. This prompted significant concern in Britain that there would be a resumption of the Anglo-French Wars and, accordingly, coastal defence arrangements were again scrutinised.

Despite the navy's enormous numerical advantage, *La Gloire* instantly rendered all the wooden sailing ships of the Royal Navy obsolete and prompted fears of invasion. These fears would have been worsened in 1862 during the American Civil War after the first actual clash between wood and iron saw the ironclad CSS *Virginia* sink the USS *Cumberland* by simply ramming it. Wooden ships had definitely been proven to be obsolete!

Inevitably, a Royal Commission was established in 1859 to review coastal defence. They recommended a vast fort-building programme to ensure the protection of the Royal Navy's dockyards. The Royal Commission gave a detailed report covering all aspects of defence along the coast from the Humber to Penzance 'which is about 750 miles long, with an aggregate of nearly 300 miles on which a landing may be effected. It would be impossible to fortify, or if fortified to defend, so extended a line of coast'.

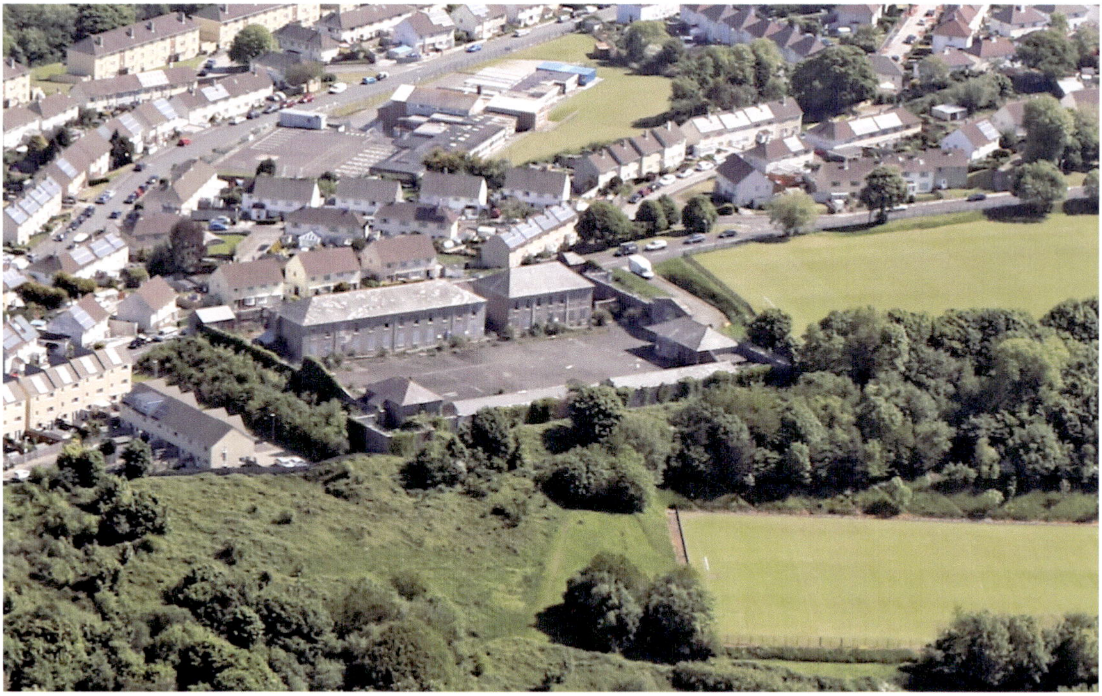

Bull Point Barracks.

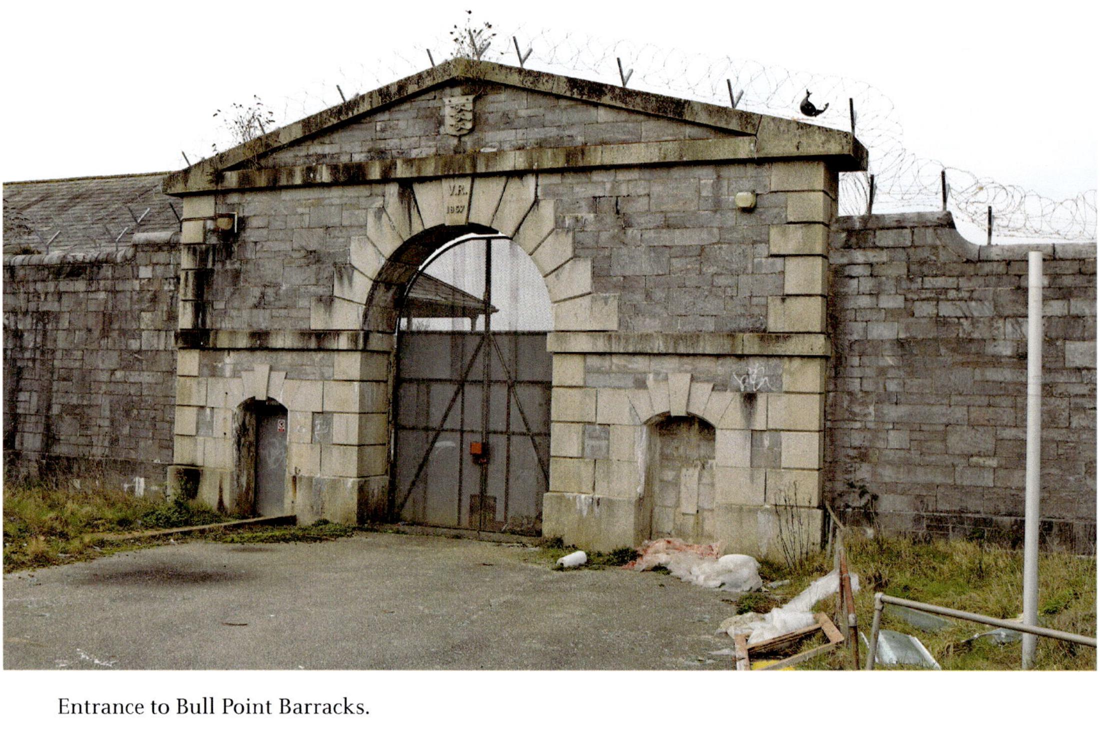

Entrance to Bull Point Barracks.

They ruled out increasing the size of the army to equal the numbers of any army likely to attack us, describing it as 'utterly impracticable'. They came to the conclusion that spending money on fortifications 'would be far more effectual for the defence of the dockyards' and 'would provide barrack accommodation for thousands of men, and would entail no future annual charge, beyond maintenance'. They also concluded that these forts could be manned by 'volunteers or militia which could not much exceed one twentieth of the cost of an equal regular force' whilst leaving 'the regular manoeuvring army ... to act with vigour in the field' which 'disposes of the objection that men are locked up in fortifications, and prevented from taking their share in the defence of their country'.

The recommendations included building rings of forts around all the naval dockyards, saying:

> We regard these Government establishments as vital points. They furnish the means of maintaining our power at sea, by the vast stores, the appliances for the construction and repair of ships.
>
> The amount of our total estimate is £10,390,000 (equivalent to £1,019,012,240 in today's money!); of which sum £1,885,000 is for the purchase of land, £7,005,000 for the fortifications we recommend for erection, £500,000 for the armament of works, and £1,000,000 for floating defences.

Floating batteries had been used, not entirely successfully, during the Crimean War. Writing in the *Royal United Services Institution Journal*, Volume 2, Issue 6 (1858), Captain Fishbourne RN said of these floating defences:

> No one who had sufficiently considered the subject could have supposed otherwise than that they would have been most difficult to navigate, of very limited utility, and would, under some circumstances, be unsafe. The results obtained from those employed at Kinburn (in the Crimea), the only occasion on which any of them have been tried, are not sufficient to warrant the many sacrifices of number of guns, of form, &c., necessitated by the great weight of their iron casing, if it does not also show that their form was not their least defect.

The following is extracted from the original report. The commission's priorities, as far as Plymouth was concerned, were:

> 1st. The defence of the entrance to the Hamoaze.
>
> 2nd. The security of the Sound as an anchorage for our own ships, and against its occupation by an enemy.
>
> 3rd. The adoption of means to prevent the bombardment of the dockyard, by the ships of the enemy at a long range.

With reference to the first of these, there are only two channels by which ships can enter the Hamoaze: passing either eastwards or westwards of Drake's Island. The channel to the west is too shallow for large warships to use.

It was generally considered that the tortuous nature of the main entrance to the Hamoaze, would effectually guard that harbour against an attack by the ships of an enemy ... This passage is already tolerably well covered by the guns in the existing batteries ... Drake's Island ... the Citadel and the Eastern and Western King Batteries.

We recommend that additional guns should be placed on Eastern King and Western King, and others on Devil's Point beyond the latter, to bear in a direction up the harbour. A battery should be constructed on or near the site of the present private saluting battery on Mount Edgcumbe, the guns of which would bear on the channels on either side of Drake's Island.

The [existing] forts at Picklecombe and Staddon Point, and the battery on Staddon Height, are all that at present exist for the defence of the entrances to the Sound ... and a work is commenced at Cawsand for the defence of the adjacent bay. The sites selected for the two first-named forts are well chosen, but the works themselves are insufficient in extent, and from their construction are entirely unfitted to resist the concentrated horizontal fire of shells, that could be brought to bear on them by large ships of war. The existing open battery on Staddon Height, from its elevated position and consequent immunity from the fire of ships, would materially assist in preventing an enemy from anchoring in the Sound. It is desirable that more powerful batteries should be constructed at **Staddon Point**, the guns bearing on the anchorage and across the eastern entrance to the Sound. On the opposite shore of the Sound a work should be constructed under the present battery at **Picklecombe**...

An open battery should be constructed on the **Hooe Lake Point**, to co-operate with the work at **Cawsand**, not yet completed, as well as with the Picklecombe Fort.

...bombarding the dockyard is, however, still possible, by vessels lying outside the breakwater towards its eastern end, from whence part of the naval establishments are visible.

We are therefore of opinion that a powerful casemated work, of such a form as to bring fire to bear in every direction, more especially to seaward, should be constructed immediately behind the breakwater, near its centre, and commanding the approach to both entrances from seaward.

We now proceed to consider the land defences. A land attack may be made upon Plymouth either from the west (Looe and Fowey) or from the east (Torbay, Start Bay, the fine harbour of Dartmouth, and the Yealm, the latter close to Plymouth).

The fortification of Plymouth to landward must, therefore, be considered under these four heads; viz.

1. The fortification of the peninsula between the St. Germain's River and the sea, which may be called the 'Western Defences.'
2. That of the country between the St. Germain's River and the Tamar, which may be termed the 'Saltash Defences.'
3. That of the country between the Tamar and the Catwater, which may be termed the 'North-Eastern Defences.'
4. That of the high ground between the Catwater and the Sound, which may be called the 'Staddon Heights Defences.'

As regards the first section ... a powerful Fort on either flank, and one minor, intervening work; the left, above **Tregantle** Farm; the right, on a hill near **Screasdon** Farm; and the centre, midway between them...

There are two places on which we consider an enemy might land for this purpose if unopposed; viz., Whitsand Bay and Cawsand Bay. As regards the former, however, the coast is chiefly bounded by high and precipitous cliffs; and the only point on which he could land is near the present coast-guard station under the village of Rame, where a **battery** should be placed flanking the beach, and protected against assault by a small work on **Knatterbury Hill** (an Historic England Scheduled Monument but unfinished earthwork, between Wiggle and Polhawn). This will also support the battery for the defence of **Cawsand** Bay. But the success of an enemy in any attempt to land inside the western defences, would result in his occupying Maker Heights, and destroying the dockyard from that position, would be so serious an event, that we consider it advisable to repair and strengthen the existing old **redoubts on Maker Heights**; we are also of opinion that it would be desirable to construct a defensible **barrack** in their rear, which would act as a support to those works and furnish troops to serve the adjacent sea batteries, and to aid in opposing any attempt to land.'

'As regards the second head, relating to the defence of the dockyard and harbour from the north-westward, we recommend that the high ground above Saltash should be occupied by **three works**; one on the hill which is crossed by the old turnpike road; another on a knoll close to St. Stephen's, between that village and the first-mentioned work; a third to the left of St. Stephen's, to act as a support to this portion of the line. A **battery, secure in itself, on a knoll** commanding the bridge which crosses the mouth of a creek running up from the River Tamar at **South Pill**. The occupation of this position would suffice for defence against artillery of the ordinary range, but would not meet the case of a bombardment by rifled guns, the ground in this quarter affording numerous views of the naval establishments; we therefore recommend that **two works** should be constructed in advance of this line, one on a commanding feature above **Burrell House** (between St Stephens's and Trematon), the other on a knoll near **Elmgate** (west of Ince Castle, overlooking the Lynher)...

We turn now to the third head, or 'North-Eastern Defences.' The only existing works of defence to landward on the eastern side of the Hamoaze are

1. The **lines of Devonport**, which have been in progress at intervals from the year 1758 to the present time. Although these works are altogether ineffectual for the protection of the steamyard at Keyham, and the victualling yard, which are outside of them, they cover the dockyard and gun wharf.
2. **Plymouth Citadel**, commenced in the reign of Charles II, and which commands the Catwater and the approaches to Hamoaze, is about 2,200 yards from the Devonport Lines; it will be a valuable support to the works on the right of the 'North-Eastern Defences.'
3. Two small square redoubts, of field profile, about 1,000 yards in advance of Devonport Lines; one on a commanding position to the north-east of the lines, called **Mount Pleasant**; the other on **Stonehouse Hill**, nearly midway between the lines and

> the Citadel. Both of these works, more especially the latter, are now much obstructed by houses ... the naval arsenal, exclusive of the ordnance magazine establishment at **Bull Point**, occupies a length of nearly two miles. To obtain a line for works which would cover the victualling yard, dockyard, gun-wharf, and steam yard, and at the same time be free from the obstruction of houses, the shortest position that could be taken up must have its left on Weston Mill Lake and its right on the Catwater...

We recommend that a work should be established on the high ground between **St. Budeaux and King's Tamerton**, and that the line should run from thence near **Burrington House**, by **Quarry Pound Tor House** (Hartley), **Mount View** (between Thornhill and Sungates), the hill near the **Wellington Villas** (Wellington Street Stoke), in front of the **Borough Gaol** (near the Guildhall!), and thence to Catdown; further, that an advanced work should be placed on **Honiknowle** that being a point upon which an enemy might establish batteries for the destruction of ships in the harbour, and of the establishment at Keyham...

We accordingly recommend that the outer line of works between St. Budeaux and Catdown, should be connected by lines of ditch and rampart, and that in rear of that line, works should be constructed on the prominent features of **Ashpark** and **Eastdown.** With the arrangement proposed, the right of the outer line will be supported by

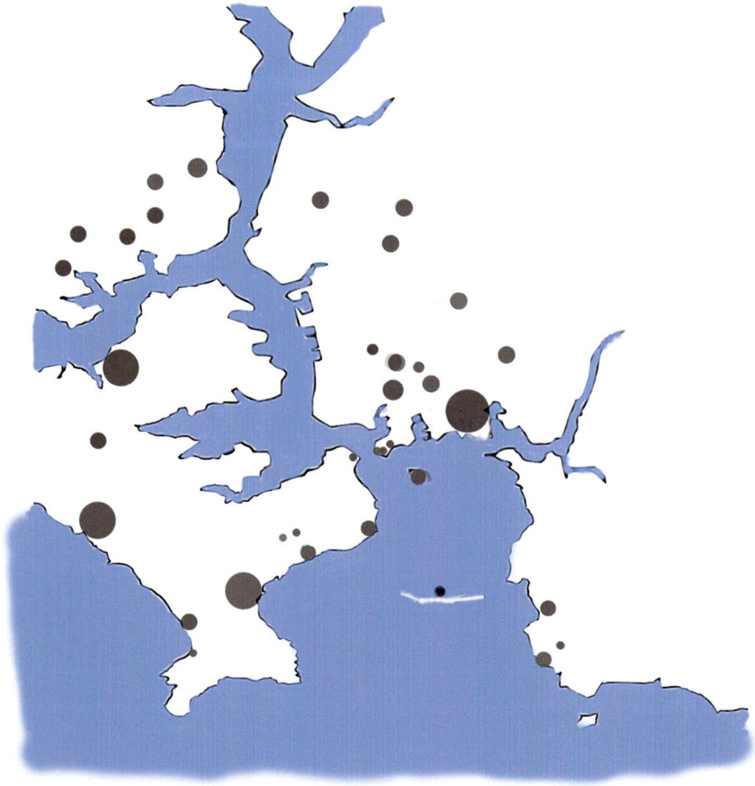

Sound map showing RC recommendations.

> Plymouth Citadel, the centre by the work at Ashpark, and the left by that at Eastdown ... it is desirable therefore that casemated barracks should be constructed in the citadel in lieu of the existing old barracks...
>
> We now turn to the consideration of the defences on Staddon Heights. From this position there is a full view of the naval establishments within bombarding range, and if occupied by an enemy, he might not only destroy the dockyard and ships in the harbour, but he would also take in reverse the eastern sea defences of the Sound, and the land defences between the Catwater and the Tamar. In addition to the necessity of preventing an enemy establishing himself on these heights, a fortified position thereon would cover the passage across the Catwater. The principal work would be on the main ridge between Hooe Lake and the valley of the King's Reservoir (at Bovisand); the other, a smaller one, on the hill immediately to westward of that reservoir.

The original recommendations were not followed to the letter, as we shall see. Sometime between 'the Seventh day of February 1860', when the report was completed, and the commencement of construction the forts around the 'Three Towns' were moved out from within the towns themselves to the surrounding rural parishes. All the Saltash works were abandoned.

The ring of forts started in Cornwall and because they were constructed outside of the built-up areas, a system of roads was built to allow access to them. They are shown on the old OS maps simply as 'Military Roads', and some are still called that today. They allowed the transport of the hundreds of tons of stone blocks and everything else needed to build such large structures in areas where the usual traffic was a farmer's wagon on a dirt road.

Working clockwise, Garden Battery in Mount Edgcumbe was built in 1862–63, Picklecombe in 1861–67, Cawsand in 1861–63, Polhawn Battery in 1862–64, Tregantle Fort in 1858–65 and Scraesdon in 1859–62.

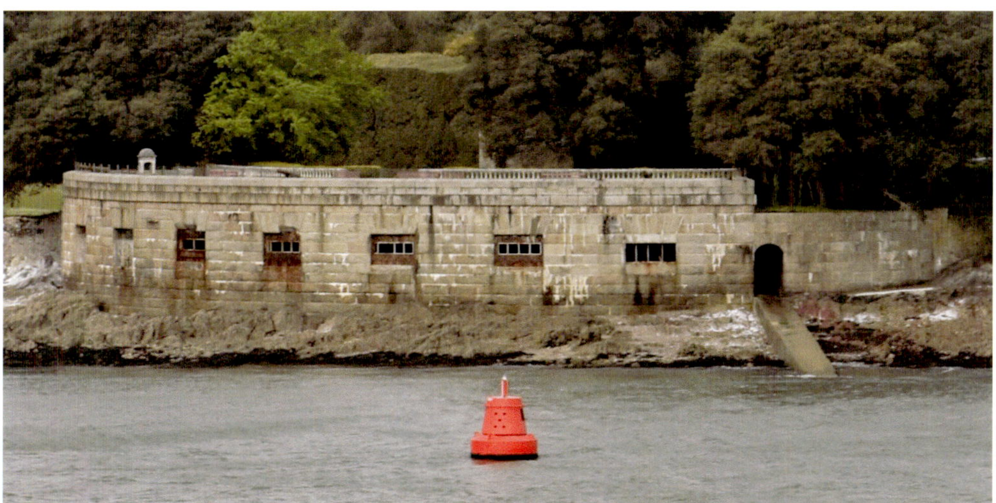

Garden Battery.

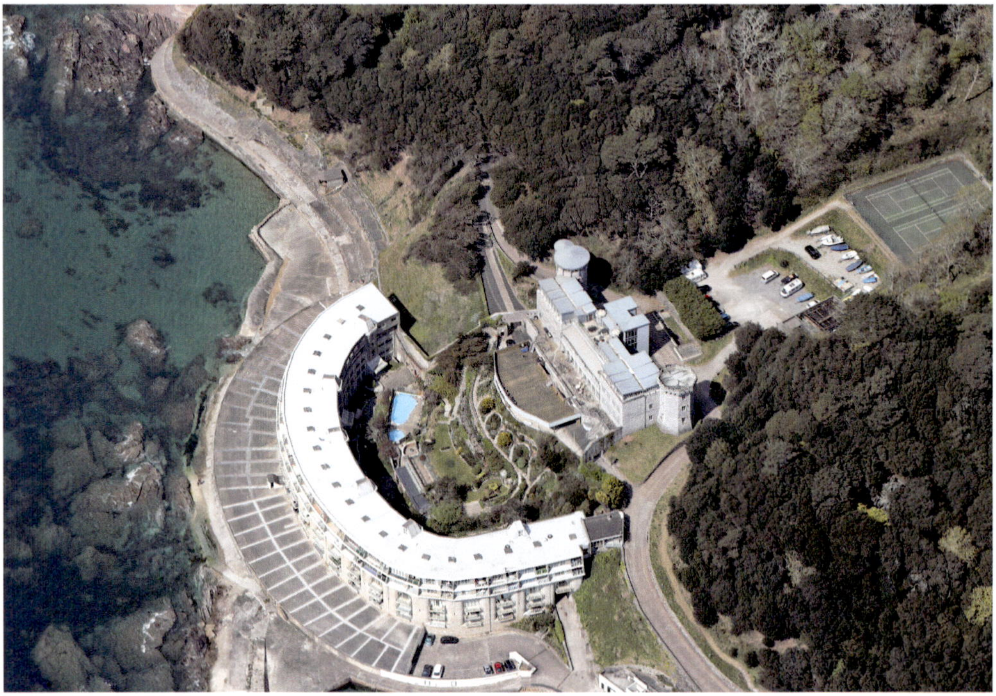

Picklecombe Fort with older barracks behind.

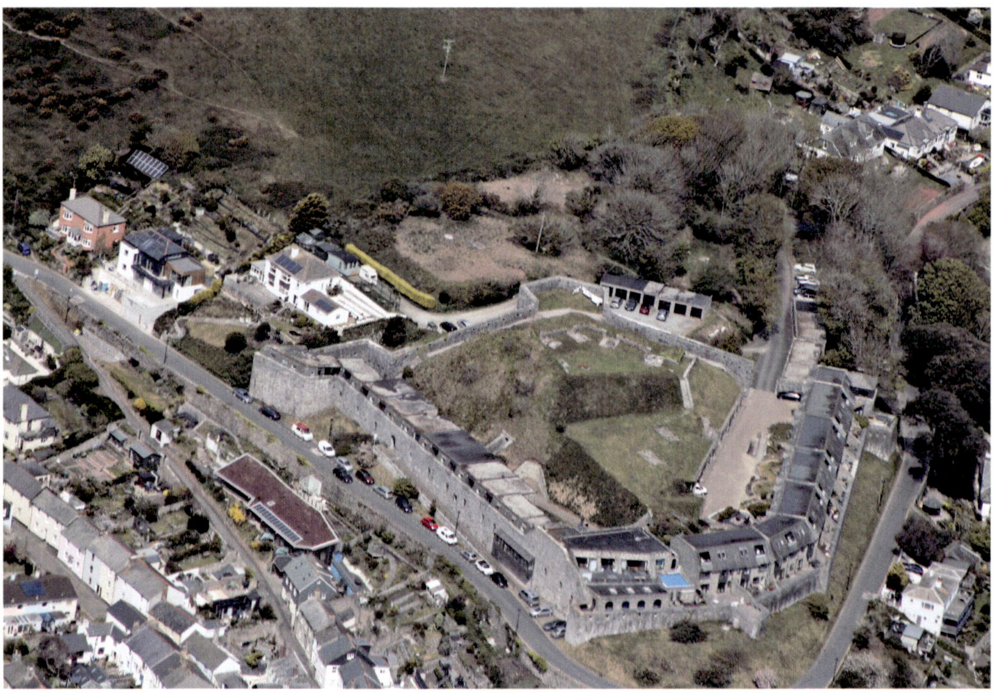

Cawsand Fort.

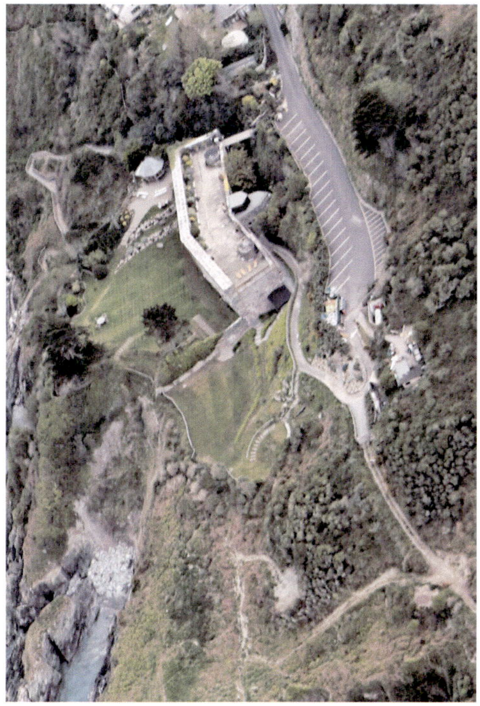

Polhawn.

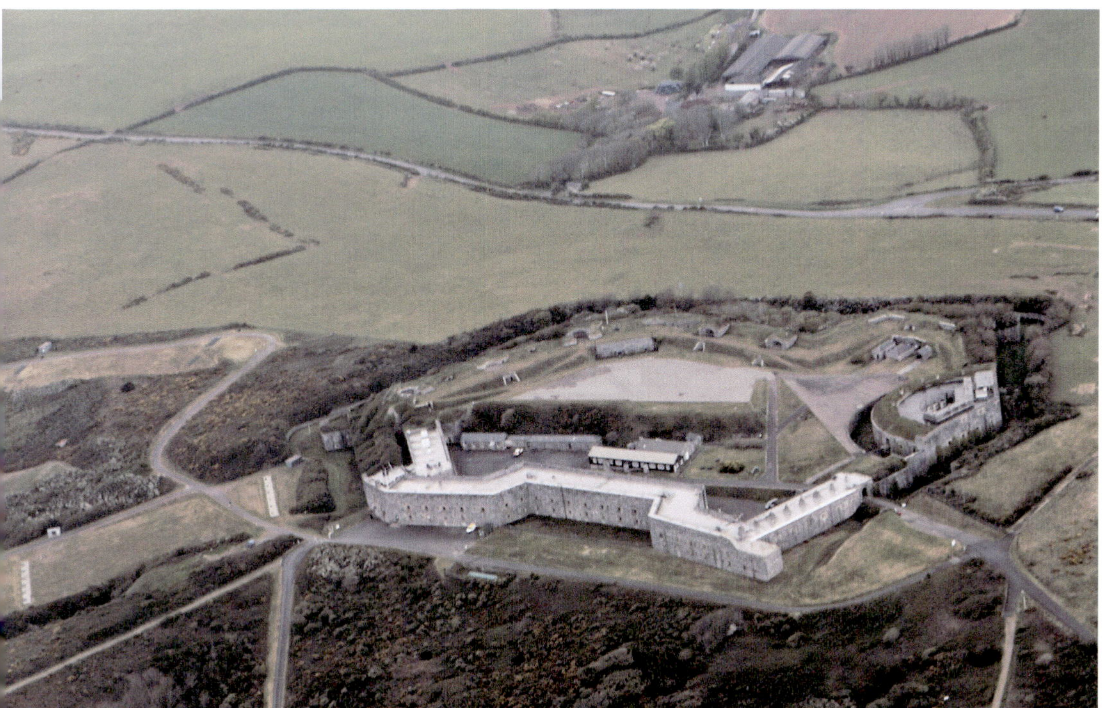

Tregantle.

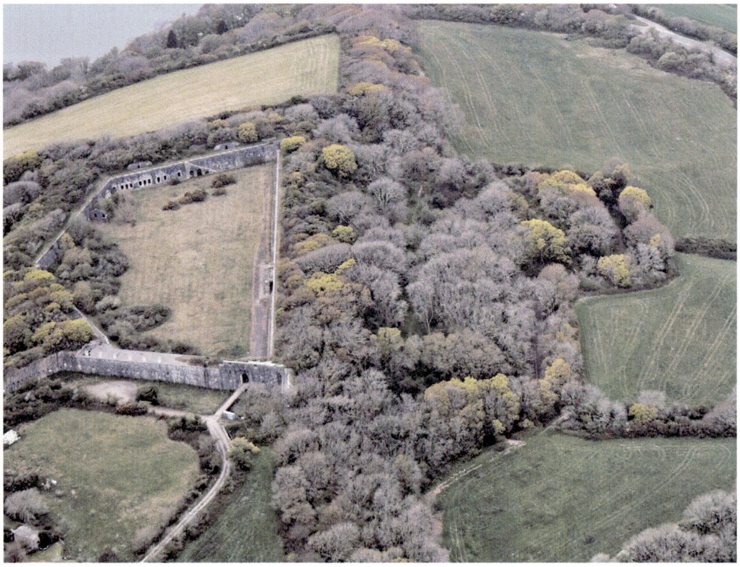

Scraesdon.

East of the Tamar were built Agaton (1863–71) and Ernesettle (1863–68) forts overlooking the river in the west, then Knowle Battery (1863–70), Woodland Fort (1863–70), Crownhill Fort (1862–69), Bowden Fort (1863–69), Eggbuckland Keep (1863–71) and Fort Austin (1863–68), then on to Efford Fort (1863–68) and Laira Battery (1863–71) overlooking the Plym in the east. Also rebuilt between 1861 and 1862 as a battery was the old Western King Redoubt, to match its partner Eastern King. The recommended new battery at Devil's Point was not built until 1901.

Continuing the line along Staddon Heights we find Fort Stamford (1861–69), Staddon Fort (1861–69), Brownhill Battery (1860–70), Frobisher Battery, Watchhouse Battery (1864–65), Staddon Point Battery (1898–99) and Fort Bovisand (1861–69). The massive wall at the end of the rifle ranges was also built at this time.

The cost for the Plymouth area alone was estimated at £3,020,000 in 1860; according to the Bank of England inflation calculator, used for all my comparisons, that equals £296,190,275 today.

In Cornwall, after roads had been constructed in the area by the War Department and all the stone had been carried by horse and cart so Tregantle and Scraesdon forts could be built, a railway was built between 1886 and 1893 from the pre-existing Wacker Quay to transport all the guns, ammunition and stores (including fresh water) needed via a turntable and an inclined plane, ending at a point just outside Tregantle now used as a car park. There was an engine shed at Wacker to house the locomotive, which pulled the trucks along the line beside the river as far as the turntable, and another at Scraesdon to house the stationary steam engine which pulled them up the inclined plane. A second locomotive pulled the trucks from Scraesdon to Tregantle. The sheds were still shown on the 1905 OS maps; indeed, I can remember the one at Wacker in the 1980s. Think how much labour it would have saved if this railway had been built before the construction began.

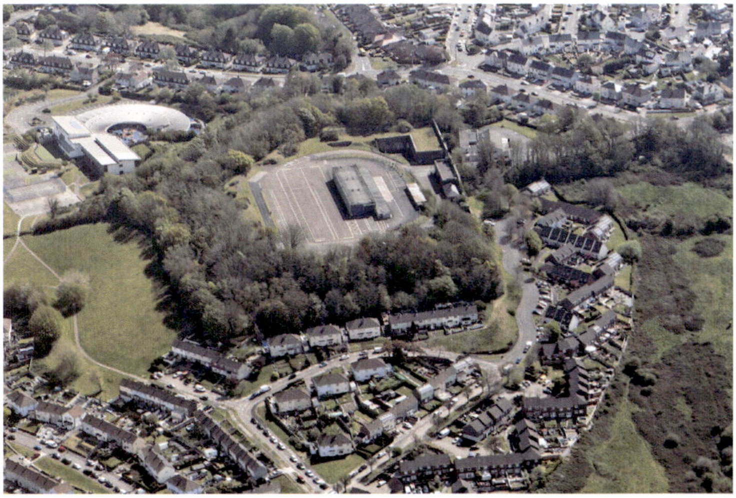

Agaton.

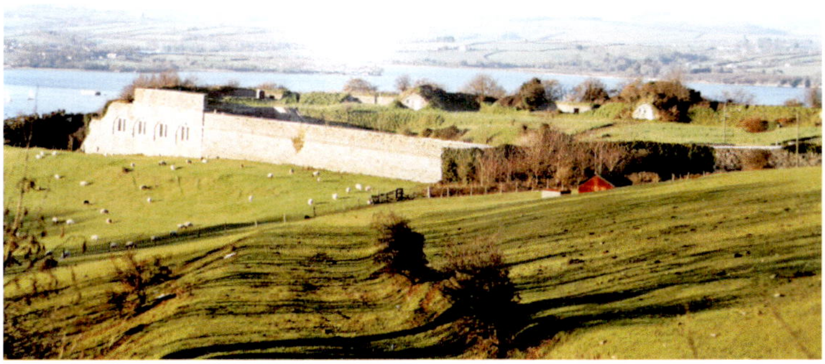

Ernesettle in the 1970s.

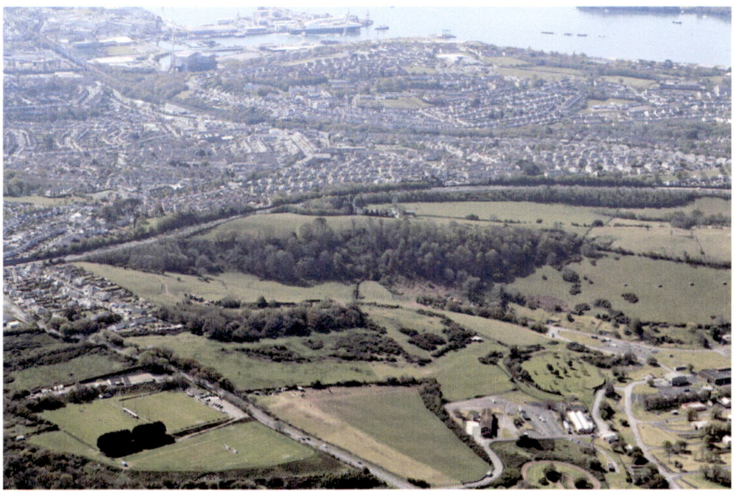

Ernesettle, now lost in trees.

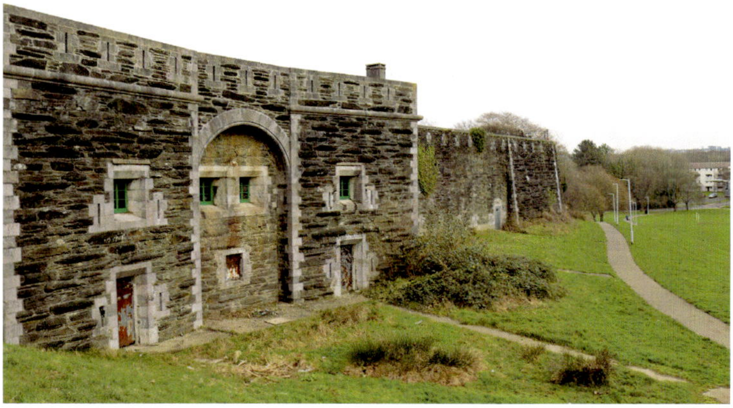

Knowle.

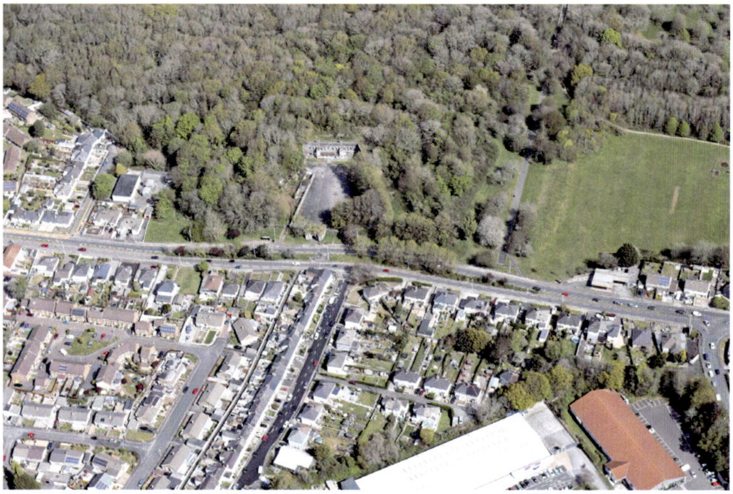

Woodland.

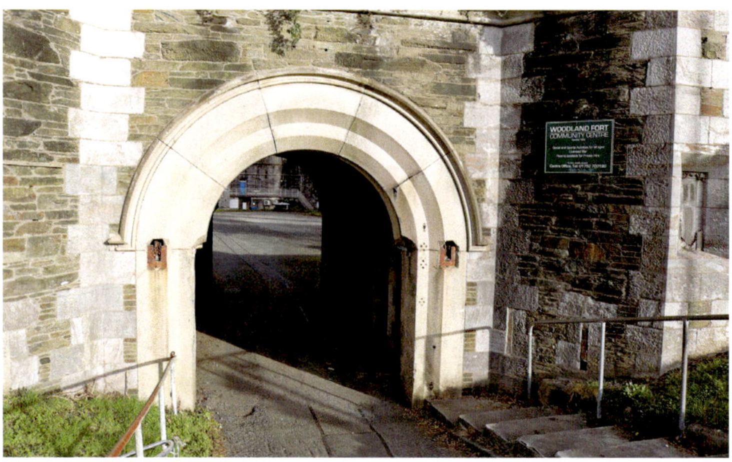

Woodland entrance.

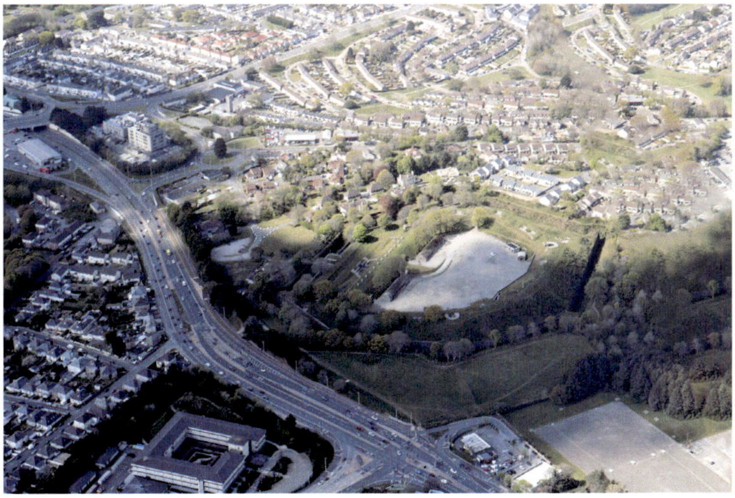

Crownhill.

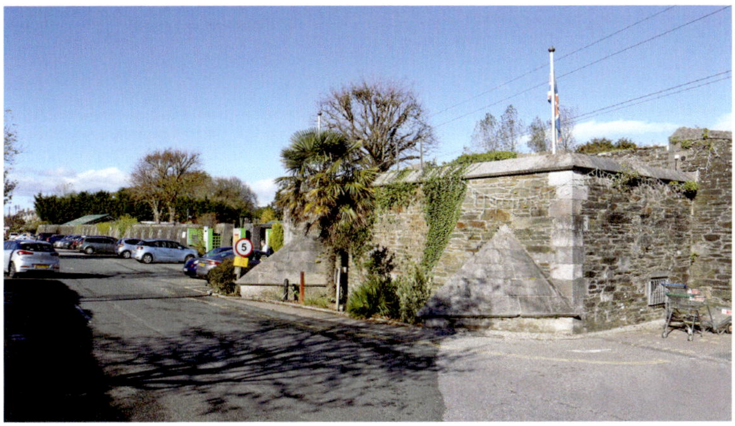

Bowden Fort.

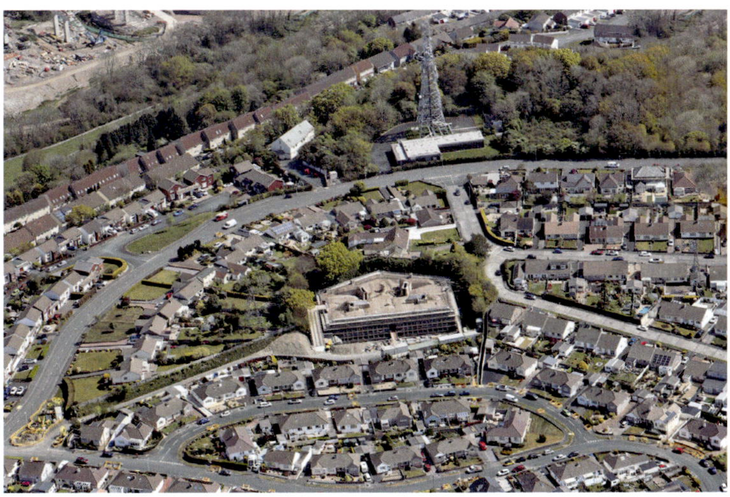

Eggbuckland Keep.

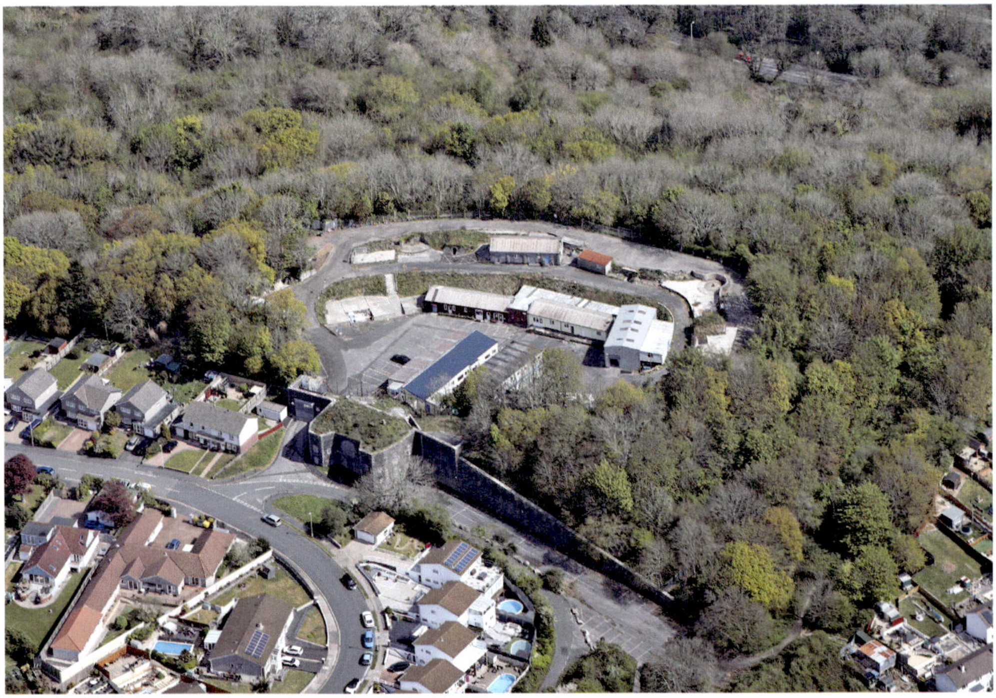

Fort Austin.

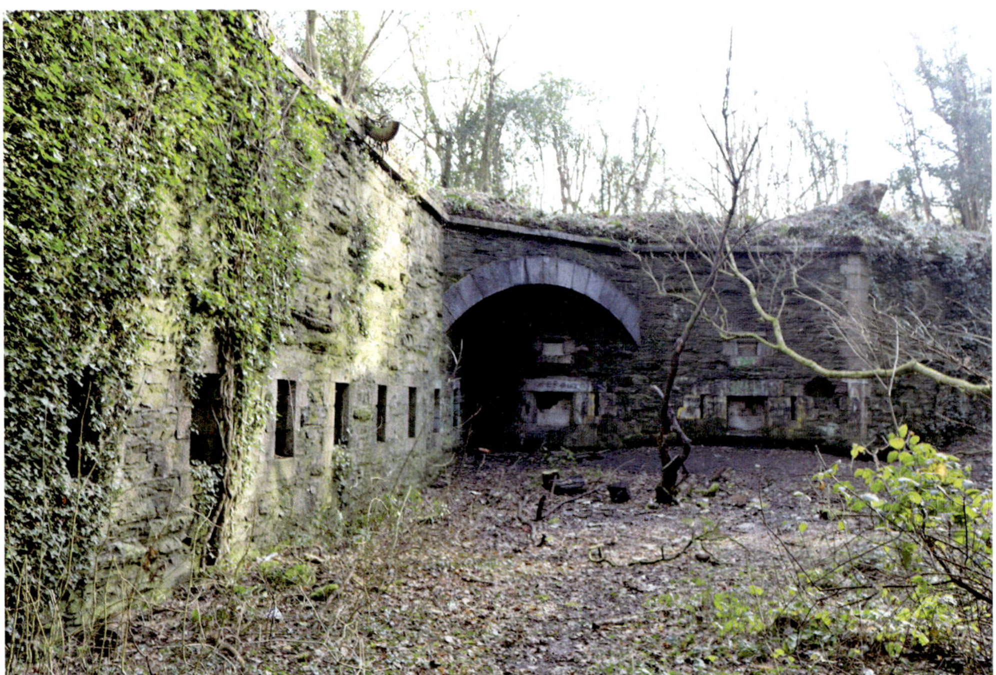

Fort Austin external defensive point in ditch.

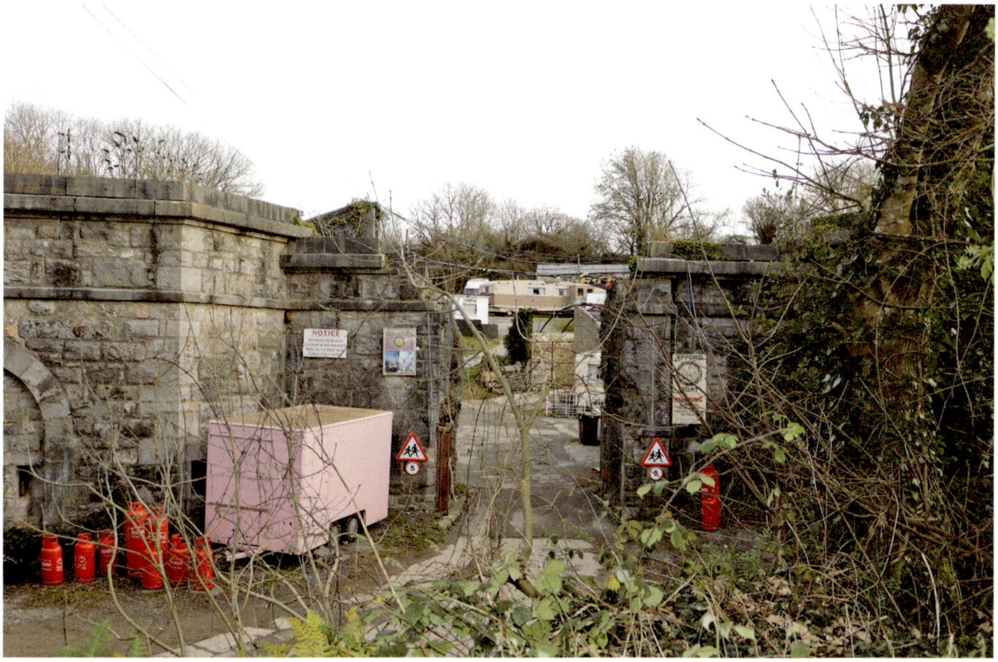

Efford Fort, now a showman's park.

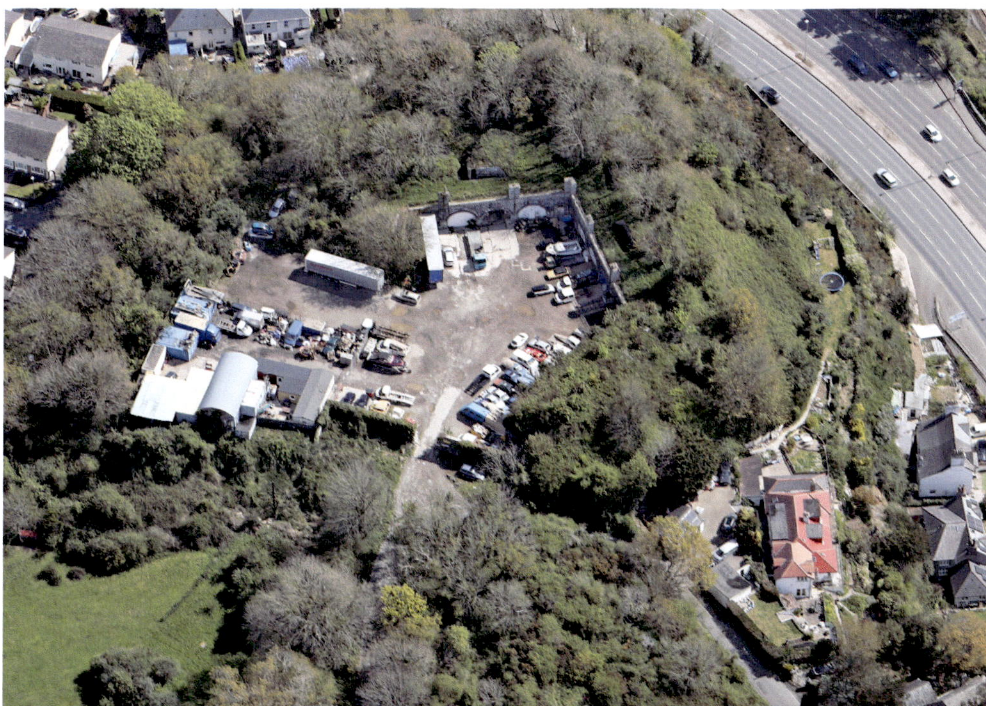

Laira Battery.

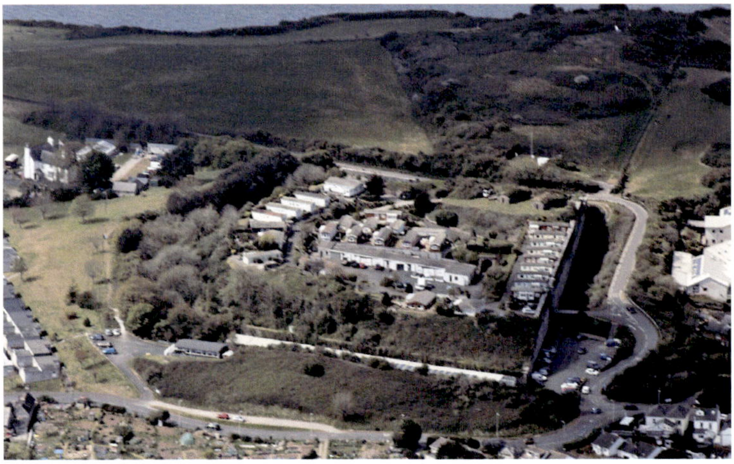

Fort Stamford.

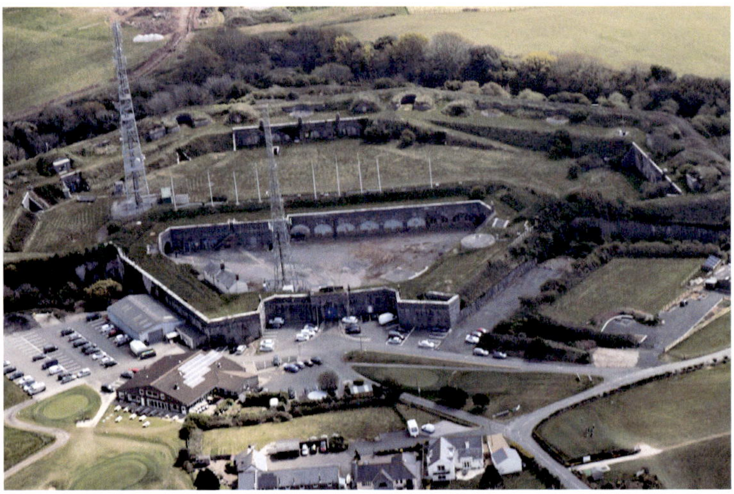

Staddon Fort.

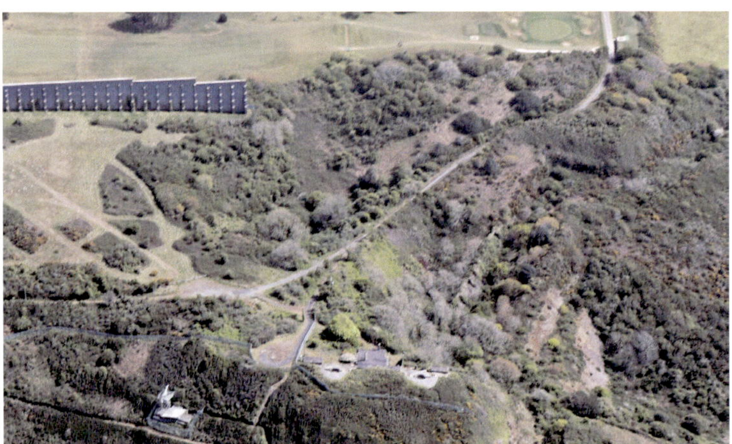

Watchouse and the remains of Frobisher batteries. Brownhill, to the top right, is out of sight.

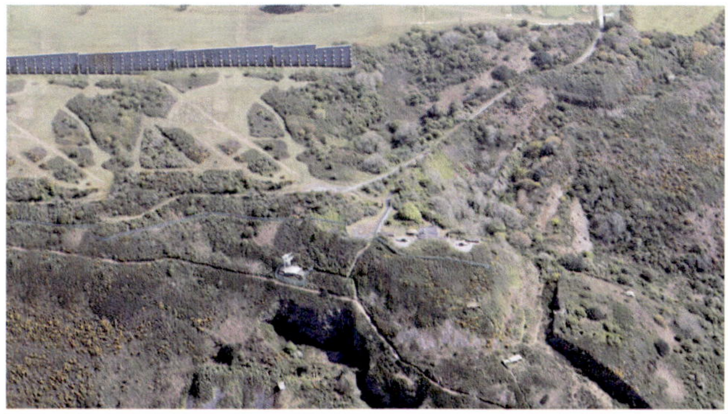

Watchouse battery with modern radar site below. The huge wall at the end of the rifle butts and defensive ditch are visible.

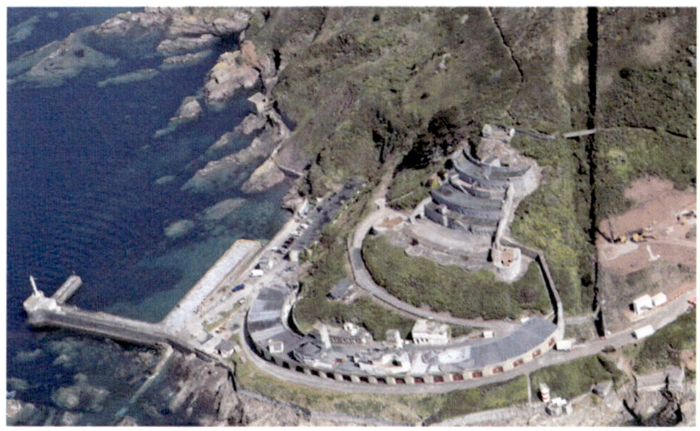

Fort Bovisand with Staddon Point Battery behind.

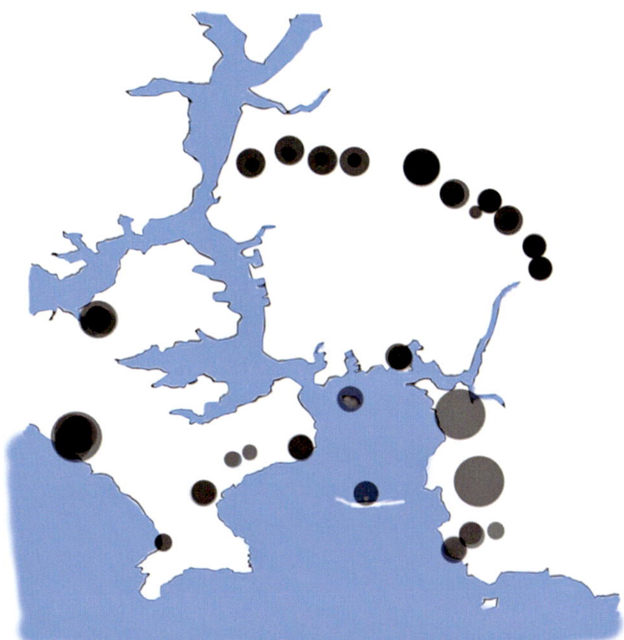

Map showing forts as built.

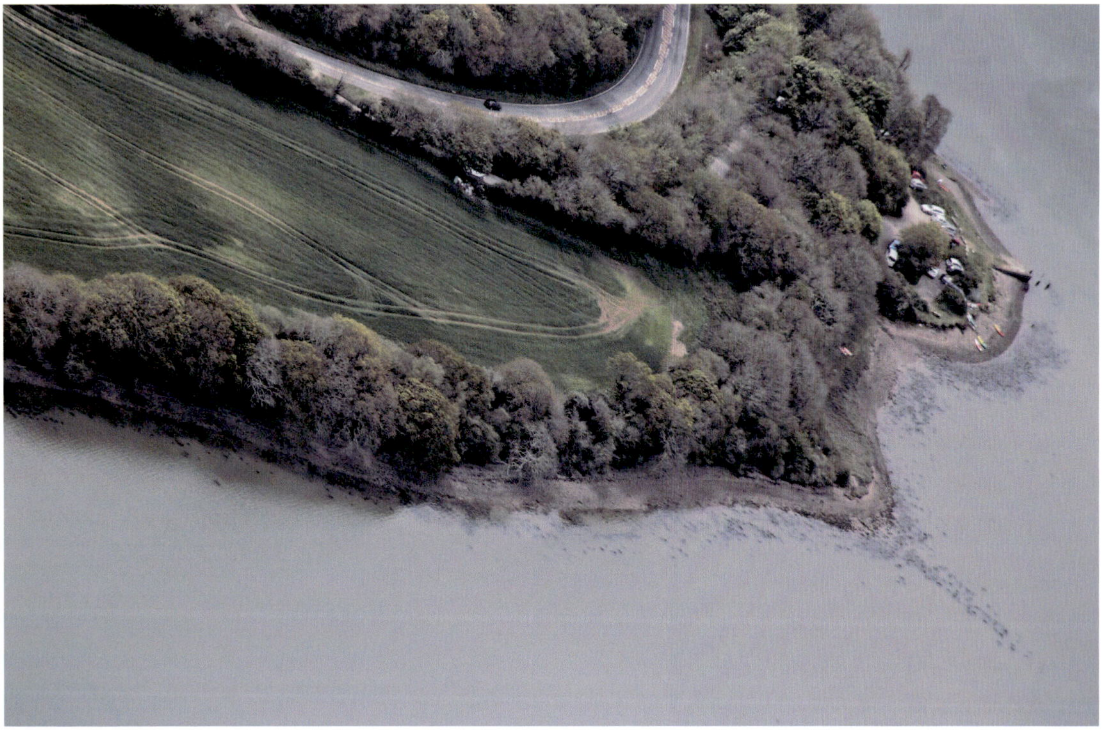

Wacker Quay and the site of the tramway.

Each of these forts was massive, with thick stone walls made mainly from limestone or granite. Being polygonal, they were the very latest in defensive technology, Many had bastions called caponiers on each corner and a wide defensive ditch around the outside. The huge walls were designed to withstand a battering from contemporary cannonballs and the defenders had covered walkways which allowed them to get to any part of the fort. From these they could fire through musket slits at anyone attempting to cross the defensive ditch to try to scale the walls and take the fort. The caponiers also housed cannon which could fire along the ditch, making it a very dangerous place to be and rendered attack by infantry almost impossible. Compared to medieval forts, which were built to protect people against attackers with bows and arrows and scaling ladders, these were impregnable.

The commission had to consider how to man all these forts given the 'small amount of force usually maintained in this country, and especially the limited number of the Royal Artillery'.

> Your Commissioners having carefully considered this question, are of opinion that the amount of training required for the ordinary service of garrison guns are comparatively of so simple a nature, that the exclusive employment of a highly trained and specially educated body of men, such as now compose the Royal Artillery, is not absolutely necessary. In fact, those portions of the course of instruction laid down for soldiers of the Royal Artillery which appear indispensable for the performance the duties

> of garrison artillery engage but 146 hours of the 663 hours course ... We feel justified therefore in expressing the belief that previously untrained men of average capacity can be taught the ordinary duties required for such service, in about a month and that in three months, such men might be made capable of performing most of the duties that are necessary for the efficient working of garrison artillery ... when supported by a due admixture of fully trained men and commanded by properly qualified officers...
>
> Our attention has been called to the employment of vertical fire against shipping, as an auxiliary to horizontal fire, and as being, with all its confessed disadvantages of want of accuracy, the most likely description of fire to be effective against stationary iron-sided vessels, at moderate distances. We have had before us a Report on this subject, lately addressed to the Secretary of State for War by Colonel Lefroy, Royal Artillery, and Lieutenant-Colonel Owen, Royal Engineers, in which it is shown that the percentage of mortar shells which may be thrown upon the deck of a vessel at anchor up to 700 yards is far from inconsiderable; and considering the very destructive effects of large shells bursting in the hold or between the decks of a vessel, we are of opinion that mortars should enter much more largely into the armament of our sea defences than is at present the case...
>
> The following table shows the comparative size of the works proposed by us in the foregoing project for the defence of Plymouth, as measured by the number of guns each is capable of mounting; the amount of bomb proof barrack accommodation to be provided, and the probable expense; the whole approximately. Neither mortars nor light guns for flanking defence and for interior redoubts, are included.

In addition to the enormous expense of the building of all these forts, there would have been the even larger long-term expense of manning and arming them. The commission's initial estimate had been £500,000 to cover armament, which was for all the forts in ten areas around the country. It seems government incompetence is nothing new.

The original proposal in the late 1860s called for the local forts to have a total of 862 guns. The vast majority of these appear to have been the not totally successful Armstrong 7-inch breech loaders or BLs, also known as 110 pounders, (186) and 64-pound rifled muzzle loaders or RMLs (102). As an example, according to the Historic England listing for Tregantle Fort:

> It was intended to house 22 breech loaders (7 inch), 13 rifle muzzle loaders (64 pounders), 10 smooth bore breech loaders (32 pounders) and 26 other mounted guns. However, it was never fully armed and by 1882 there were only six gunners in a fort equipped for 1000. One gun was fired, experimentally, in 1886.
>
> The fort was used as an infantry barracks as early as 1891. The associated rifle ranges were built in the early 1900's following its change to an infantry battalion HQ. After 1918 it was virtually abandoned before being re-opened in 1938

The total number of guns in the area in 1899 came to 302, with eighty-seven by then mainly obsolete 64-lb RMLs and just fifty-six of the planned 186 Armstrong 7-inch breech loaders, which were by then unpopular. Many of the proposed 68-lb RMLs were seemingly replaced by 32-lb RMLs.

Position	Work	No of Guns	Barrack Accommodation	Expense
SEA DEFENCES	Picklecombe	40	200	
	Staddon Point	32	180	
	Breakwater	100	600	
	Hooe Lake Point	10		
	Drake's Island	30	180	
	Eastern King	10		
	Western King	15	50	
	Saluting Battery Mount Edgcumbe	10		
	Whitesand Bay	10		
	Knatterbury Hill	5	100	
		262	1,310	375,000
SALTASH	Main Work	30	300	
	St. Stephen	20}		
	Left Work	15}	200	
	South Pill	5	50	
	Burrell House	30	300	
	Elmgate	30	300	
		130	1,150	500,000
North—eastern Defences	St. Budeaux	40	500	
	Burrington House	20	200	
	Quarry Pound	30	300	
	Tor House	15	150	
	Mount View	40	500	
	Wellington Villa	15	150	
	Borough Gaol	30	300	
	Cat Down	15	150	
	Three advanced Works in front of line	25	300	
		230	2,550	1,200,000
Inner Line	East Down	30	500	
	Mount Pleasant	10	100	
	Ash Park	30	500	
		70	1,100	350,000
Staddon Heights	Main Work	30	400	
	Other Work	20	200	
		50	600	200,000
Maker Heights	Barracks		300	25,000
Connecting Lines between Tregantle and Screasdon				20,000
TOTAL for PLYMOUTH		742	7,010	£2,670,000

Station	Guns		Barrack Accomodation, chiefly bomb-proof		Expense of Works including purchase of land	
	No.	Total	No. of Men	Total		Total
PLYMOUTH						
Recommended by Royal Commission	742		7,010		2,670,000	
In works in progress	120		1,000		350,000	
		862		8,010		3,020,000

Table showing Plymouth fortifications as recommended by royal commission.

Taking the personnel proposed for each fort, they would have needed over 8,010 men, although they seemed to assume this would include a few skilled men (Royal Artillery men) plus members of the local militia and even volunteers. The Royal Commission had dismissed the idea of doubling the size of the army on grounds of cost, but if all the planned forts throughout the land had been built, armed and manned as originally intended, that would have been the outcome. They concluded that the total number of men needed in time of an expected attack was 15,000. In fact, these totals were trimmed down; the total listed in the 1901 census for these forts was 778. Before the building of these forts there had already been an existing total of 2687 army personnel who had been living in the various barracks and the Citadel, according to the 1841 census.

As if all these forts and batteries weren't enough, three emplacements were added to the eastern end in 1869 – Deer Park, Efford and Laira – to fill in the gaps around Efford and Laira. Presumably they were countering any chance of an invasion from Plympton.

The Deer Park Emplacement was apparently originally intended to be armed with four 64-pounder RMLs, but it was (and still is) a simple earthwork embankment with no fixed positions. If it had been needed, the plan was to arm it with guns from the nearby Efford Fort. The emplacement had a view over the valley which now includes the Parkway.

Efford Emplacement was another earthwork constructed to fill the gap between Efford and Laira forts, and stood on a bridge-like wall behind their joint defensive ditch. Six gun positions were shown on the contemporary maps, which in 1885 were home to six 8-inch RML howitzers. Having been constructed on a limestone bridge, this structure still

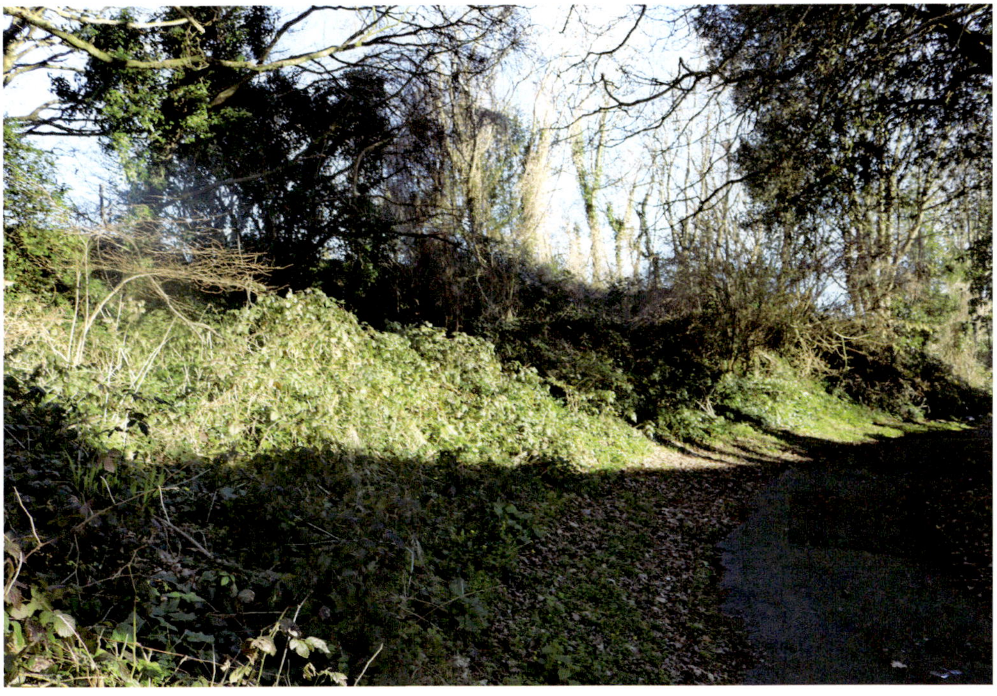

Deer Park Emplacement.

exists with its tunnel, which was built to be a sally port but now allows a public footpath to get from Crabtree to Efford. The entrance to the magazine is easily visible inside the upper end of the tunnel. There is little left on top to show the earthwork gun positions. The emplacement had an unrestricted view over the Marsh Mills area. It is scheduled by Historic England as a Site of National Importance.

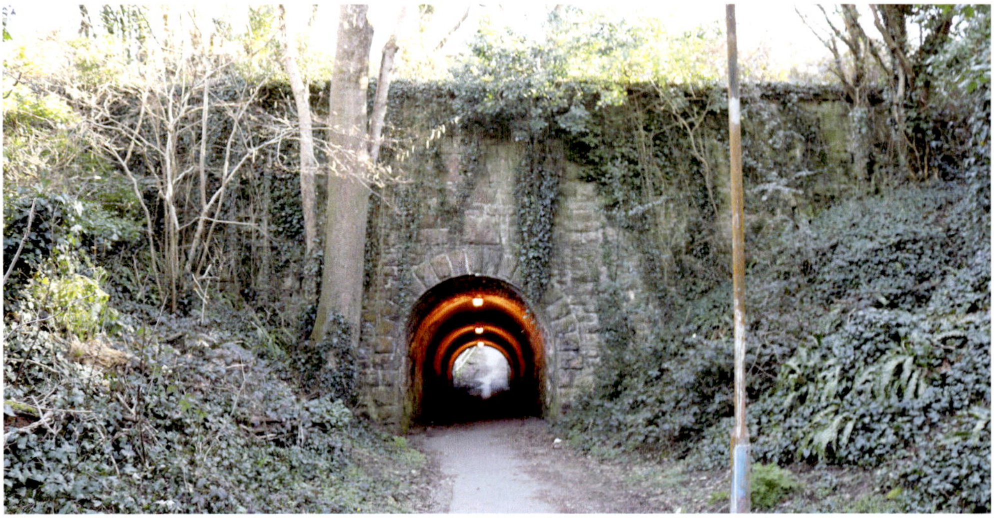

Site of Efford Emplacement.

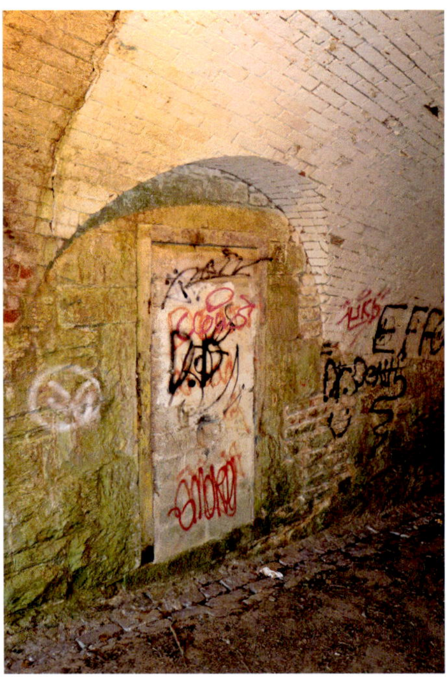

Efford Emplacement magazine entrance.

Laira Emplacement was constructed to cover the river to the west of Laira Fort, and it has a beautiful view across that area and Saltram beyond. Originally intended for six guns, in the 1890s it was listed as having four 8-inch RML howitzers. This is the best preserved of the emplacements, its layout being still clearly visible and the eastern magazine entrance being open, although the southern magazine has been covered over.

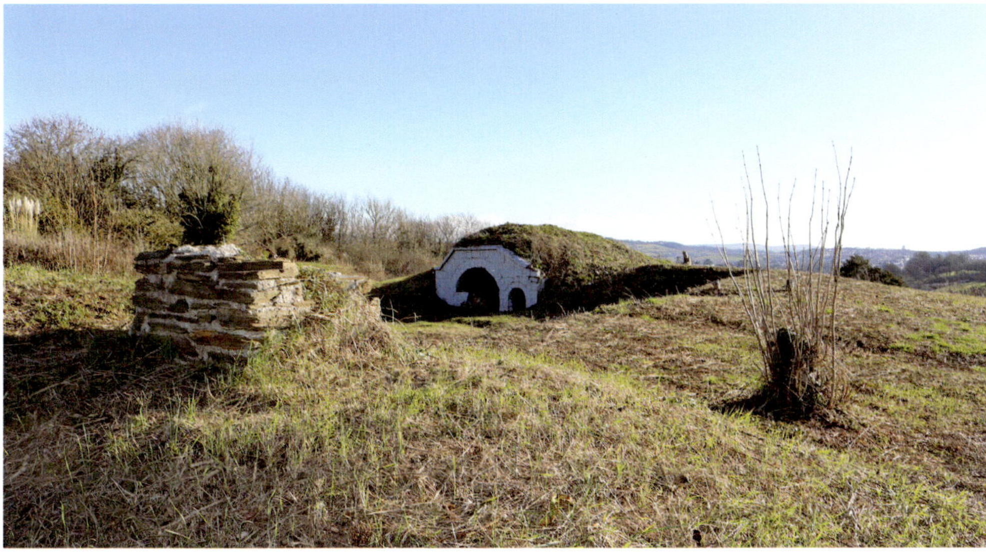

Laira Emplacement.

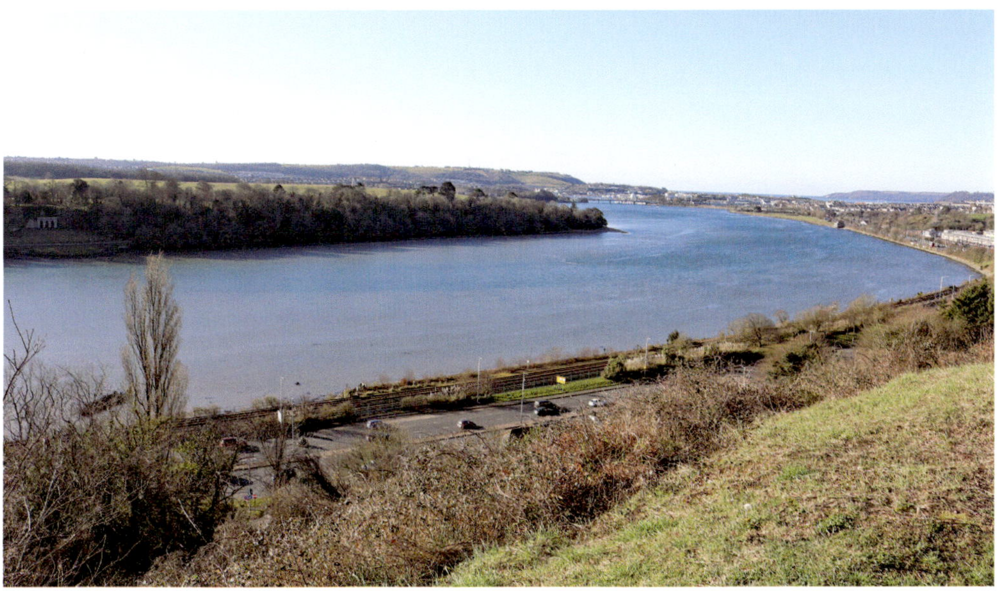

View from Laira Emplacement.

Of all these forts and batteries, three in the north-east – Fort Austin, Bowden Fort and Forder Battery – never appear in any census between 1881 and 1901. The north-eastern forts were the last to be completed and perhaps by that time economies were already needed, not least because there were not sufficient trained soldiers to man them fully. Woodland Fort appears in 1881 with only civilian occupants – nine in total. The following census, 1891, is the only time so far it shows as being manned with soldiers. There is a barrack labourer and his wife, a corporal RA, four gunners RA and seventeen boys RA – forty-one people in total. The fact they were using boys to man the fort shows how the economies were biting.

As well as all these land-based forts, plus of course the possibility of using naval ships for defence, Plymouth had the option of having defences right in the middle of the Sound.

The Breakwater Fort (1862–70) was originally conceived by the Royal Commission as a powerful casemated work, mounting 100 guns with accommodation for 600 men to protect the anchorage inside Plymouth Breakwater and close the gap between the batteries at Bovisand and Picklecombe. This original grandiose plan was for an oval fort on four tiers with thirty-three guns each and two tiers of granite gun casemates protected behind iron shields and a further seven guns on the roof. Work started in 1861, but experiments showed that only an iron structure would give sufficient protection against fire from the latest heavy RMLs. As such, the plans were altered to one of two storeys with room for sixty to 180 men, with stores and magazines on the lower and eighteen heavy rifled guns in casemates on the upper, entirely protected from direct fire by iron.

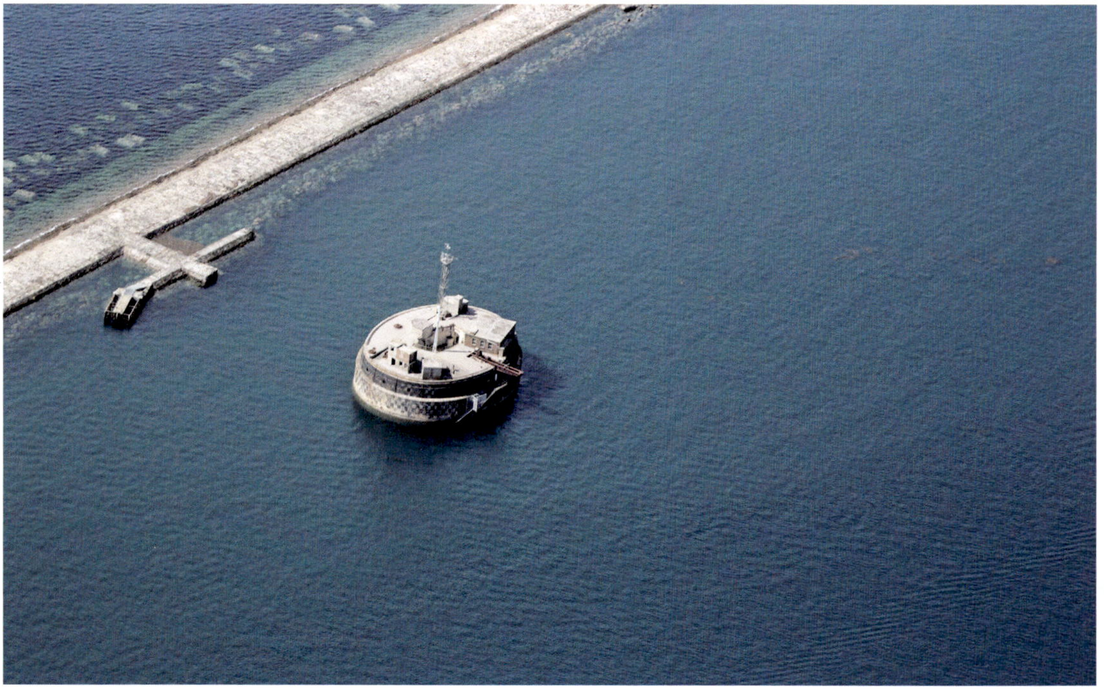

Breakwater Fort.

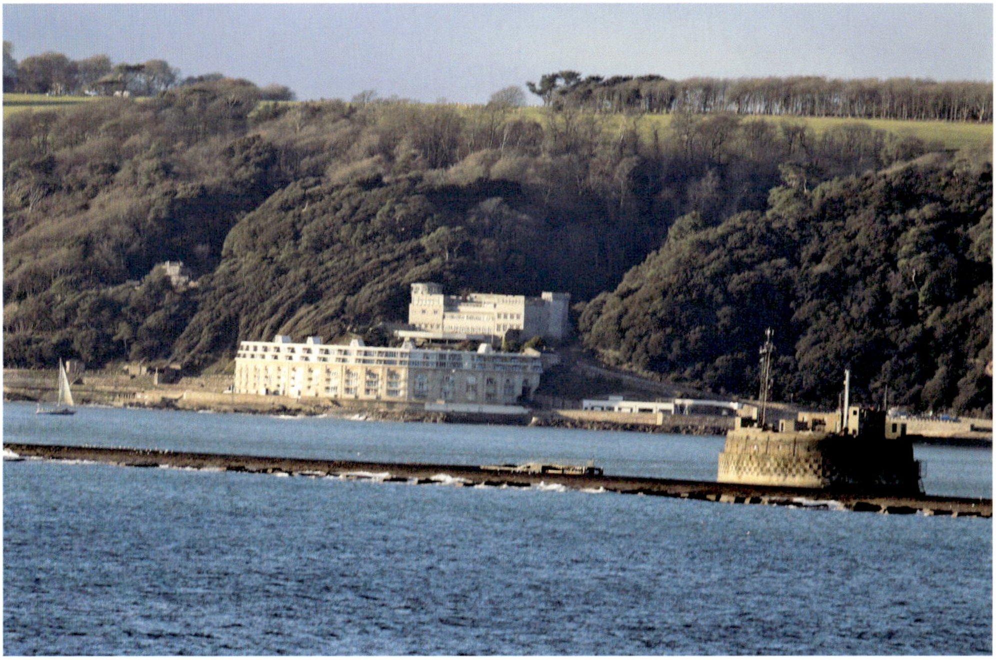

Breakwater Fort halfway between Bovisand and Picklecombe.

The fort stands 100 yards inside the centre of the Breakwater in six fathoms of water. In 1875 the armament was approved as fourteen 12.5-inch RMLs to cover the sea in front and the channels on either side, with four lighter 10-inch RMLs to cover the anchorage at the rear. These were fitted in 1879, and the fort was fully armed in 1880. According to the only census records I could find for the fort, in 1901 there were eight men there and in 1911 just two.

By the early twentieth century a searchlight was installed on the roof, supplemented by another in 1911. Although the fort was disarmed by the First World War, the searchlights were still operational and it served as the Port War Signal Station throughout the war.

The position of St Nicholas or Drake's Island just off the Hoe and at the entrance to the Hamoaze meant the island was armed from Tudor times. Drake himself was Governor of the Island in 1584, and doubtless its defences date from that time. According to Ian Hogg's *Coastal Defences of England and Wales* in 1805 it had twenty-two 32-pounder and six 18-pounder cannon. Ian Hogg says: 'The work at that time, so far as can be gathered, was an open battery with masonry embrasures.' Following the Royal Commission's report, Drake's Island was to be rebuilt (1860–64) as a granite casemated work for twenty-one guns. This was later changed to the existing design with iron, as used on the Breakwater Fort, after which 9-inch RML were provided.

In 1978 work carried out by Plymouth Corporation unearthed four RMLs on the island – three 11 inch and one 12 inch. The 12-inch RML of 25 tons was mounted on a replica carriage built by Plymouth Corporation under the direction of Colin Carpenter. It was test-fired on 22 November 1983 using 22 pounds of pebble powder, shattering nearby windows.

The island was disarmed in 1947 and used for training until 1963.

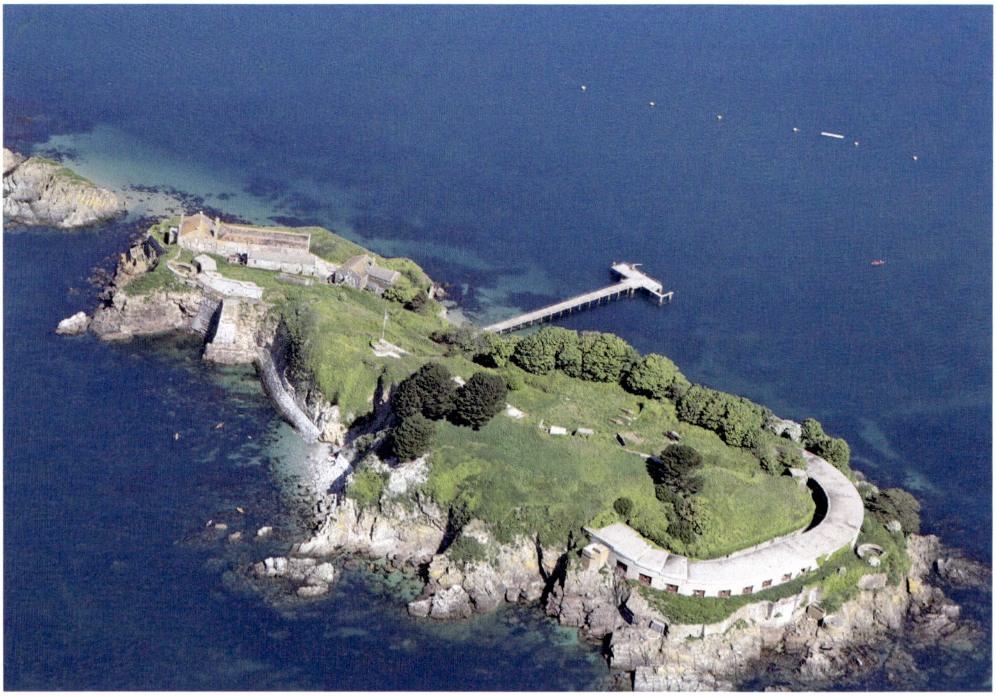

Drake's Island with RMLs on the highest point.

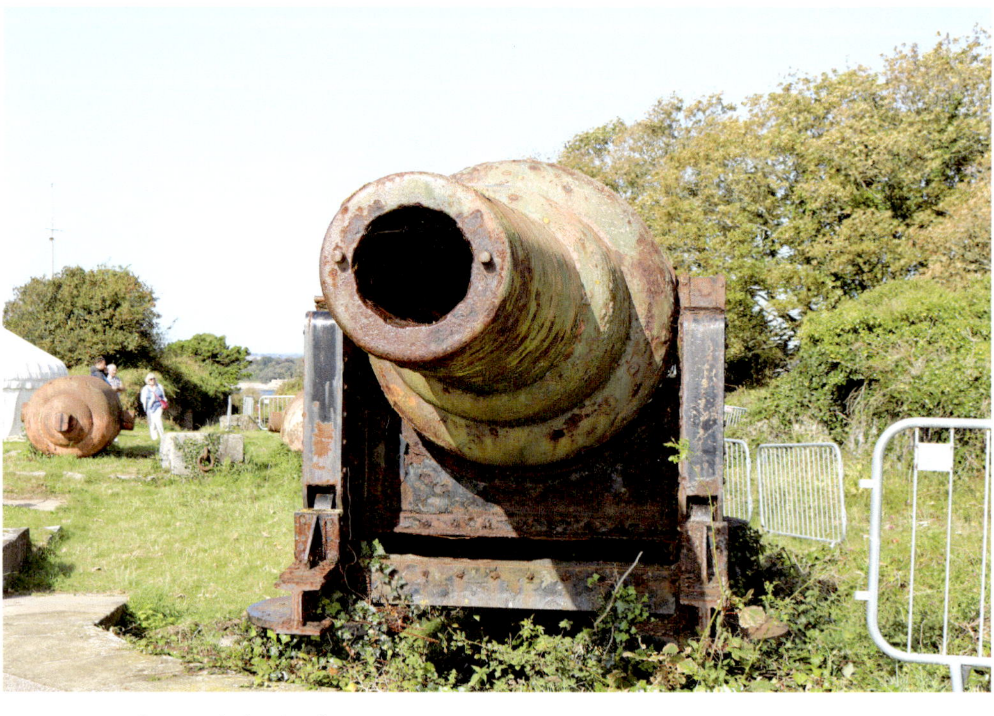

RML mounted on Drake's Island.

Artillery Developments

Whilst the fort-building programme was ongoing during the 1860s and early 1870s, developments in artillery continued that were particularly relevant to the sea defences.

Unlike previous eras where defences had been situated around the entrances to Sutton Pool, Millbay and Stonehouse harbours, development of long-range artillery meant land defences needed to occupy the higher ground, whilst the building of the Breakwater (1811–48) meant the sea defences needed to be further south than before.

The practice of rifling (machining spiral grooves inside the cannon's barrel) was done more frequently by 1855 as it gave projectiles gyroscopic stability which improved their accuracy and also meant that, unlike the spherical balls, the front part of the shell was guaranteed to hit the target. This meant that contact fuses and high-explosive shells became possible, which were much more effective than a simple cannonball. There had been earlier, unreliable experiments with hollow balls and slow-burning fuses, lit by the hot gases of the propellant charge, which exploded when the fuse burnt through rather than when they hit something. The first British Naval impact fuse appeared in 1861.

One of the earliest rifled cannon was the breech-loading Armstrong Gun, which boasted significantly improved range, accuracy and power than earlier weapons but reports of problems with the breeches of the gun, and their higher cost, meant the gun was rejected in favour of modified rifled muzzle loaders, which were basically the old cannons with rifled barrels but were capable of piercing the ironclad's armour.

Essentially, all the new forts had been designed around using muzzle-loading cannon to defend against attacks from other muzzle-loading cannon. Once the problems with breech-loading had been solved, plus the high-explosive shells with impact fuses that could now be fired, these improvements moved artillery forward by a huge amount. Long-range guns and howitzers could now lob high-explosive shells over the enormously thick walls and kill the forts' inhabitants. There was no longer any need to smash the walls and storm the fort.

Loading a RML in a confined space such as an armoured casemate was slow and the black powder originally used produced large amounts of smoke, which would not easily clear in such a confined space. By the 1870s Moncrieff 'disappearing gun' mounts were being used, a counterbalanced mounting that enabled the rifled muzzle loader to be fired in an open pit instead of inside a casemate. The gun was loaded down inside the pit where the gunners were safe, then cranked up, aimed and fired. The recoil would usually be enough to swing the gun back down for reloading, failing which it had to be cranked down. Whichever, it was still a slow and laborious process.

The defences had originally been designed to protect Plymouth and the dockyard from landward attack. Building these forts was largely complete by 1869, and a number of additional and modified defence positions, such as the emplacements previously named, had been added to the original plans by then. These defences were joined by military roads and protected by glacis slopes, ditches and embankments, forming an integrated defensive system. The defences on Staddon Heights were deployed with heavy guns to prevent bombardment and attack of the city (and the defences themselves) from the south and east.

1875–1900

For centuries naval personnel had lived and trained in hulks, old ships anchored in the Hamoaze opposite the dockyard, but by 1886 the Royal Navy had a shore base in Devonport as well, which increased the number of forces personnel in the area. It took until 1889 before men were transferred from the last depot ship, HMS *Royal Adelaide*. The RN barracks were given the name HMS *Vivid*, which it held until 1934 when it became HMS *Drake*, the name by which it is still known today.

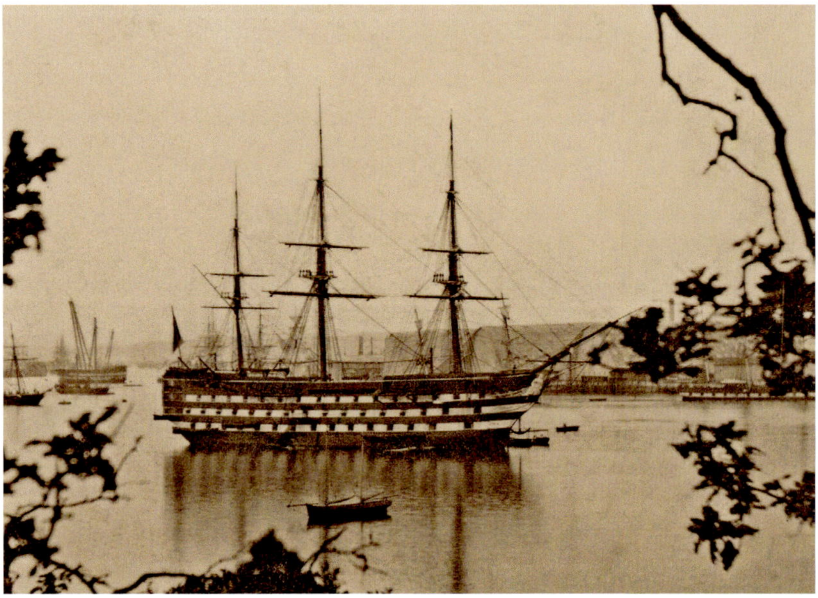

HMS *Impregnable* training ship in the Hamoaze, *c.* 1861. (George Wilson of Aberdeen)

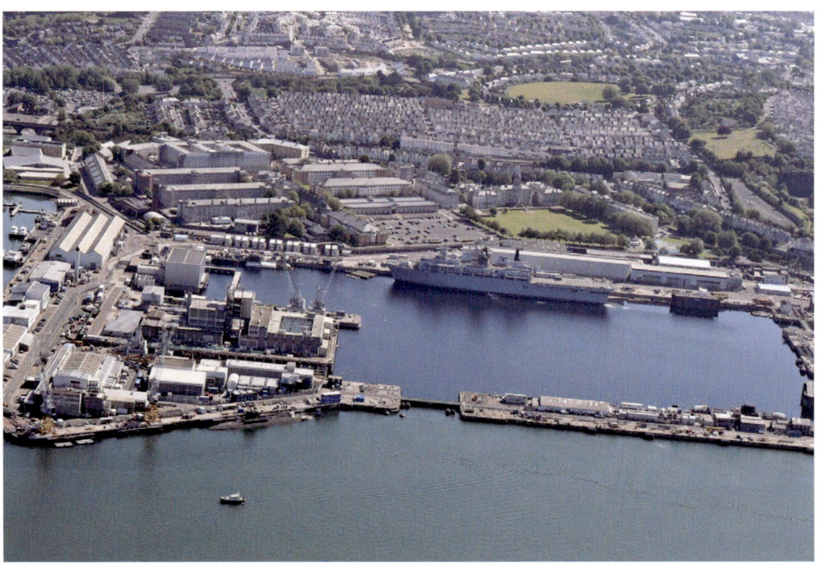

HMS *Drake* beyond No. 5 Basin.

With all these additions, the total number of military personnel shown in the 1901 census is 4,717 – over and above those in the forts.

Advances in munitions had made the forts obsolete. By the time all these fortifications were finished, Napoleon III, the cause of all this expense, was living in exile in London, having been captured during the Franco-Prussian War. Despite this, in the 1880s and 1890s the government spent even more on modernising the defences. The newer defences were mainly armed with 9-inch,12.5-inch and even 13.5-inch RMLs on high-angled mounts giving up to 70 degrees of elevation, which, given their height above the sea, would allow for long range. The shells from these guns would be dropping onto ships in the approaches or in Whitsand Bay, causing massive damage and smashing through decks, as foreseen in the original report. Again, such guns could be installed in pits, leading in the 1880s and 1890s to the open high-angle batteries built upon clifftops, which could be used to bombard ships far out to sea, and because of the height advantage they would be out of range for return fire from the enemy. These include the three emplacements around the Effort and Laira area. Also, by the 1880s more modern 'smokeless' gunpowder improved the situation.

However, it was ultimately the development and mass procurement of heavy breech loading weapons that made casemated forts completely obsolete. Such guns were ideal for open batteries and this effectively became the standard from the late 1880s onwards. As artillery ranges continued to improve, new coastal defence batteries were built around Plymouth Sound to extend the range of the guns out to sea. In the west new High Angle batteries were built at Tregantle, Whitsand Bay, Rame Head, Penlee and Maker Heights, including Maker, Grenville (the old No 4 Redoubt), Hawkins and Raleigh batteries during the 1890s. Tregantle Down Battery was built on the storage area at the end of the above-mentioned railway from Wacker Quay, what is now the Tregantle car park.

In late 1884 HMS *Defiance* became the Devonport torpedo and mining school for the navy, moored in the River Lynher between the Antony estate and Wearde. It was the first of seven ships to bear the name Defiance between then and 1955, when the school moved to Portsmouth.

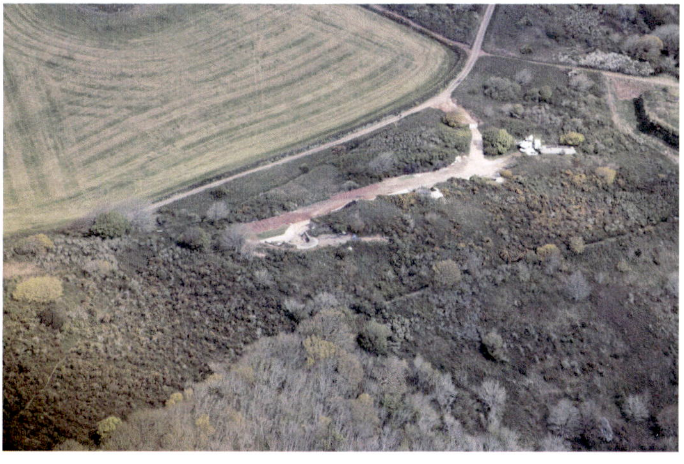

Maker Battery.

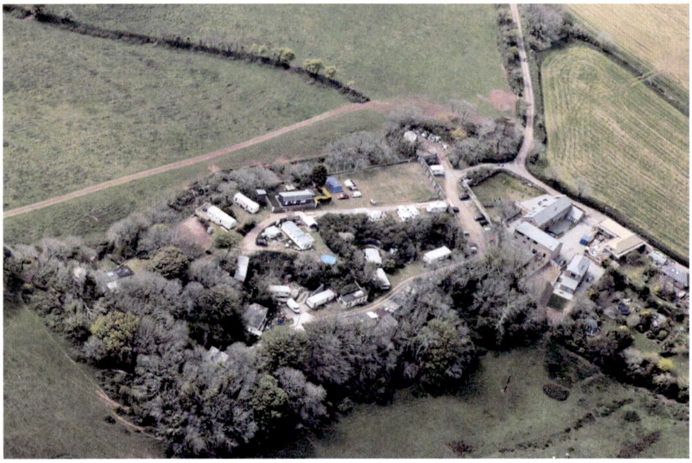

Hawkins Battery. Raleigh Battery is nearby but overgrown.

Pier Cellars was built as a torpedo training base in 1888/9 on the site of an old fish cellar. When it was first mentioned in the 1891 census, the only inhabitants were a 'Royal Artilleryman' and his family. It was usually manned by Royal Engineers, however, with eight men there in 1901, reducing to five in 1911. According to the Royal Engineers Museum, Pier Cellars was one of only four places in the British Isles (plus one in Hong Kong and two on Malta) that was armed with the amazing wire-guided Brennan Torpedo. This seems like the sort of technology used during the world wars, but in fact it was designed in 1876. In 1895 a battery was added to protect the site, as was a searchlight a year later.

Despite having all these little-used (or even unused) forts laying around, the War Department built two new soldiers' accommodations near Crownhill Fort at the end of the nineteenth century. These were then known as Crownhill Hutments, built in the 1880s but first appearing in the census of 1891, and Crownhill Barracks, which were built in 1891. The hutments appear to have been used as general accommodation for unmarried men, while the barracks were partly as married quarters. In 1891 the hutments housed 135 members of the Royal Artillery, only one of whom was married – to the cook at the officers' mess. By 1901 they housed just twenty-eight members of the Royal Engineers, including farriers, carpenters, blacksmiths and transport drivers.

The barracks first appeared in the 1901 census of Plympton St Mary. It was partly in the civil parish of St Budeaux and partly in Eggbuckland. The Eggbuckland entry shows 182 single men, about 40 per cent listed as Bombardier Militiamen (fulfilling the Royal Commission's intention that much of the defences could be manned with militiamen) and the rest Royal Warwickshire Fusiliers. The St Budeaux entry shows 120 people in total, twenty-nine married infantrymen and their families.

As previously mentioned, Elphinstone Barracks became a depot of the Royal Engineers in 1893. The census showed it was home to 156 members of the regiment in 1901, falling to eighty-five in 1911. It was apparently designated a 'magazine' and it was used to store guncotton. It was used in the manufacture of sea mines, which could then be loaded directly on to ships.

A further advance in artillery technology came with the breech-loading, quick-firing gun during the 1880s. These combined the ease of breech loading and having the charge in a brass cartridge with its own firing system. This resulted in much faster loading and firing, enabling them to engage the faster-moving vessels, like torpedo boats, which were then appearing. During the 1890s many of the existing forts were equipped with them, including Fort Picklecombe, Garden Battery and Staddon Point Battery.

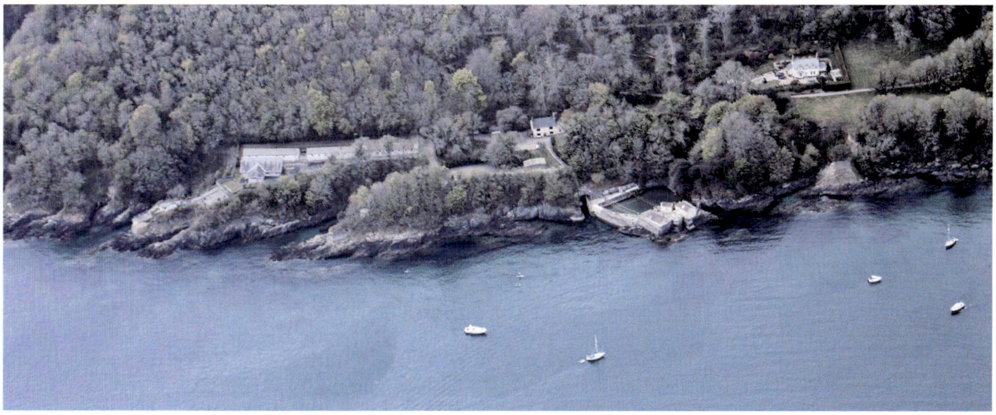

Pier Cellars.

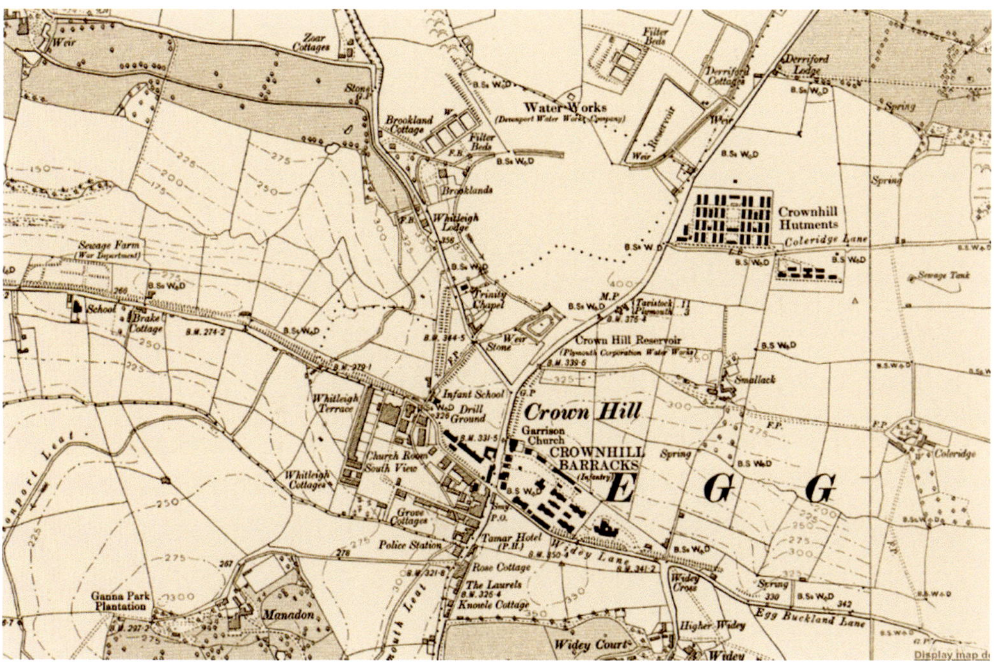

Map showing Crownhill Hutments and Barracks. (Reproduced with the permission of the National Library of Scotland, CC-BY 4.0)

6. The World Wars

After the chaotic, enormously costly and ultimately futile fort building of the nineteenth century, the new century started comparatively quietly for the Plymouth area. There were wars going on, of course, there is almost always a war going on somewhere, but they were all far away from Plymouth. They included the Boxer Rebellion in China, the Boer War in South Africa and the Spanish-American War. None of them threatened the safety of Plymothians or required the construction of defences.

As we know, this state of affairs didn't last long. Although, even the First World War little affected the citizens of Plymouth directly, unless they were in the armed forces or worked in the dockyard, which was kept very busy. We were too far from the action to be directly affected by enemy attacks by air or even by sea.

There were still a few leftovers from the previous century that were being built in the early years of the twentieth century. Near Wembury, two more coastal batteries were built between 1905 and 1909, although they really finish telling the story that I started in the last chapter. These were Lentney and Renney batteries, sited to defend the eastern side of Plymouth Sound. They were equipped with 6-inch (Lentney) or 9.2-inch (Renney) breech-loaders, long-range guns that remained in service until the Second World War.

Also built at this time was Lord Howard's Battery. It is likely that only a few people have heard of this one, but it was located overlooking Jennycliff Bay – the remains of the emplacements are still there in front of the Jennycliff Café. Recommended in 1905 and complete by 1909, this battery was equipped with two 6-inch breech-loading guns and manned by personnel from nearby Fort Stamford. It was intended to protect merchant shipping at anchor in Jennycliff Bay and the approach channel to the east of Drake's Island.

The First World War

During the First World War all these guns that ringed Plymouth and the Sound were very useful for defence, even though they were never actually called upon to defend the area for real.

Many of the old Napoleonic-era forts were repurposed for use during the First World War. I am well aware that accurate data on military sites is not easy to find. In many cases guns would have been mounted, found not to be effective and moved elsewhere with little or no record kept. Much of the data used here came from the now defunct Victorian Forts website, cross-checked as far as possible with local records. I won't guarantee it is accurate, but it is a close as I can get.

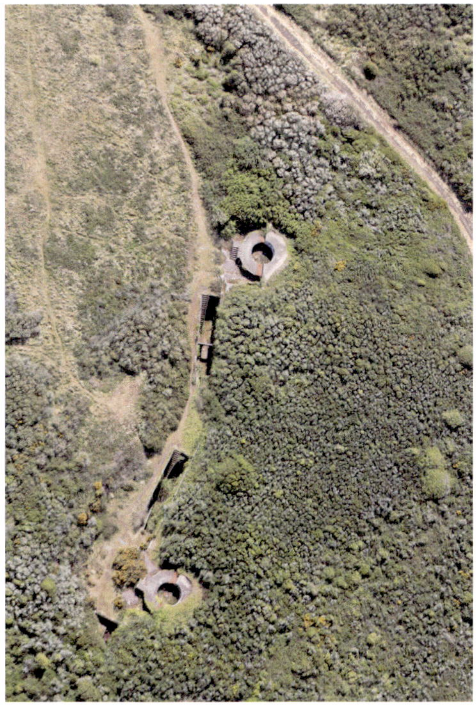

Lentney Battery.

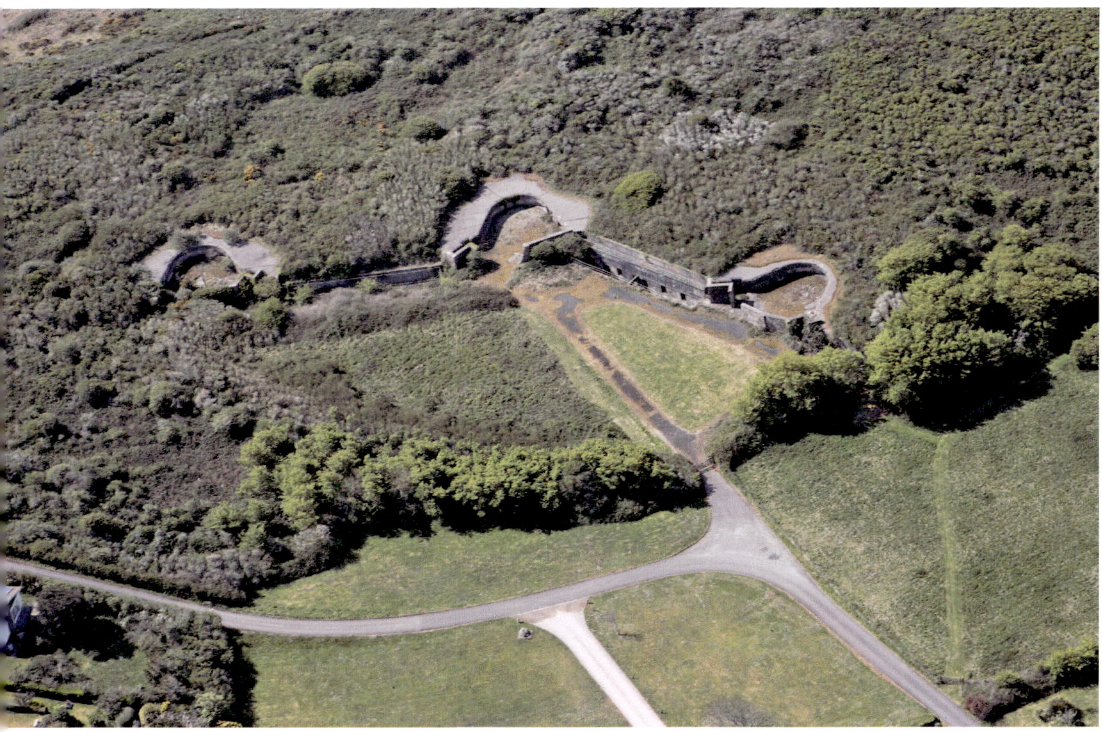

Renney Battery.

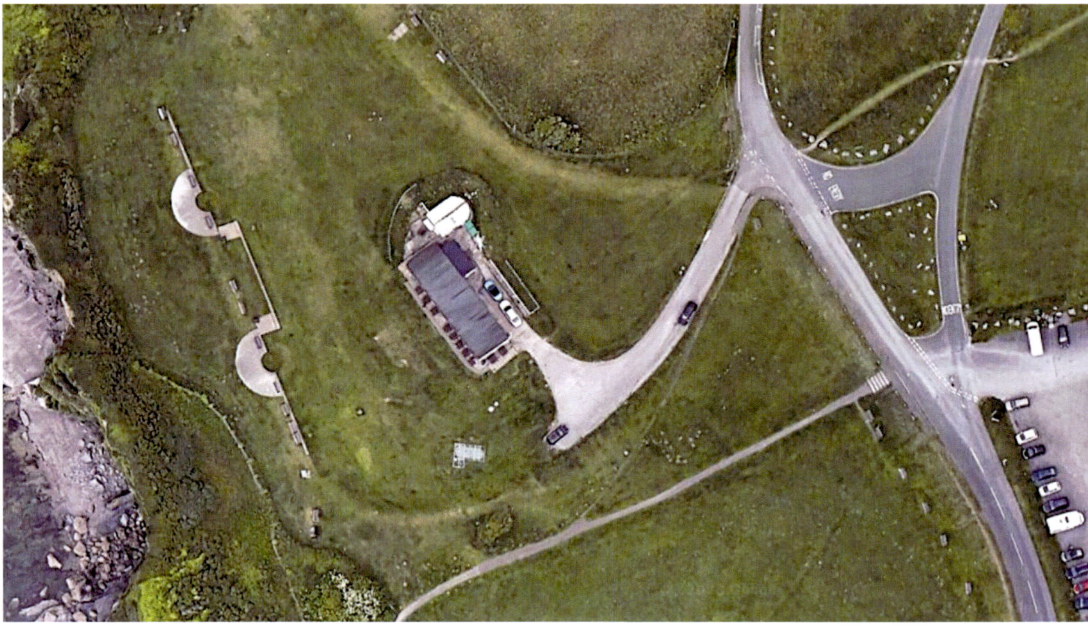

Site of Lord Howard's Battery at Jennycliff.

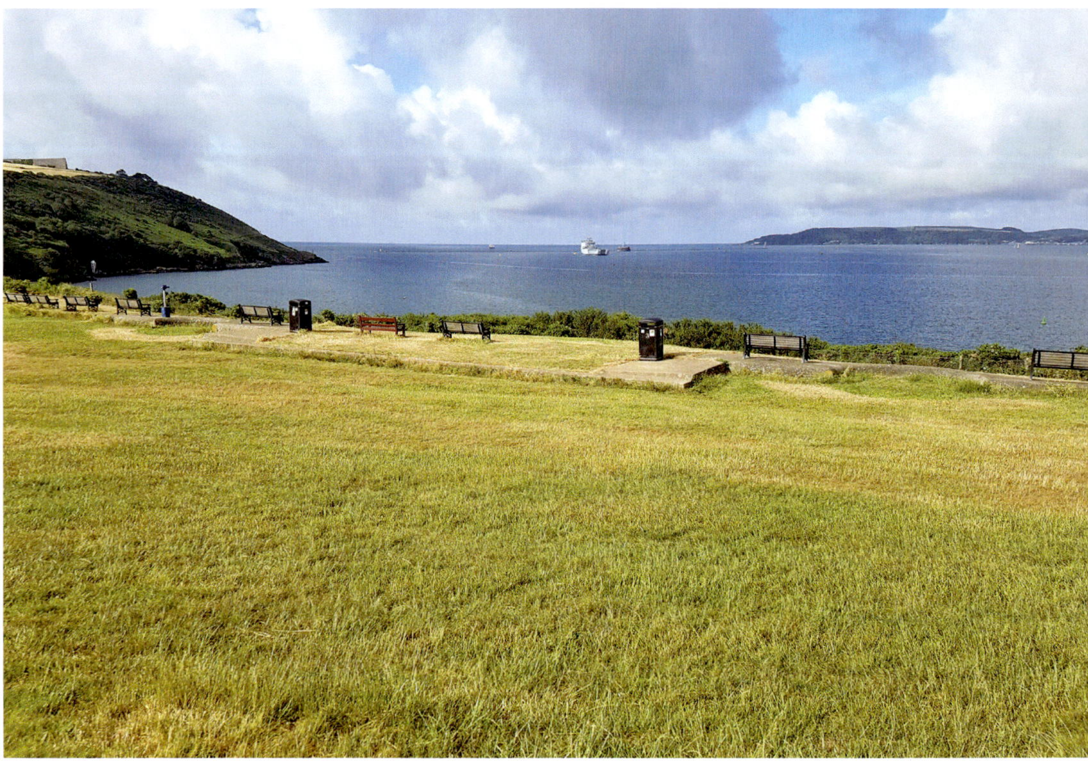

Remains of Lord Howard's Battery in front of the café at Jennycliff.

Agaton

Used as the main Royal Army Service Corps depot supplying the south-west for both world wars.

Breakwater Fort

Two searchlights had been installed between 1903 and 1911. Although the fort was disarmed by the First World War, the searchlights were still operational and it served as the Port War Signal Station throughout the war.

Cawsand Fort

Remained in military occupation during the First World War, although the guns had all been removed by 1903.

Crownhill Fort

The fort was used during the First World War as a recruitment and transit depot for troops en route to their Turkish and African fronts. After the war it was used as a demobilisation unit.

Devil's Point

One 12-pounder gun remained.

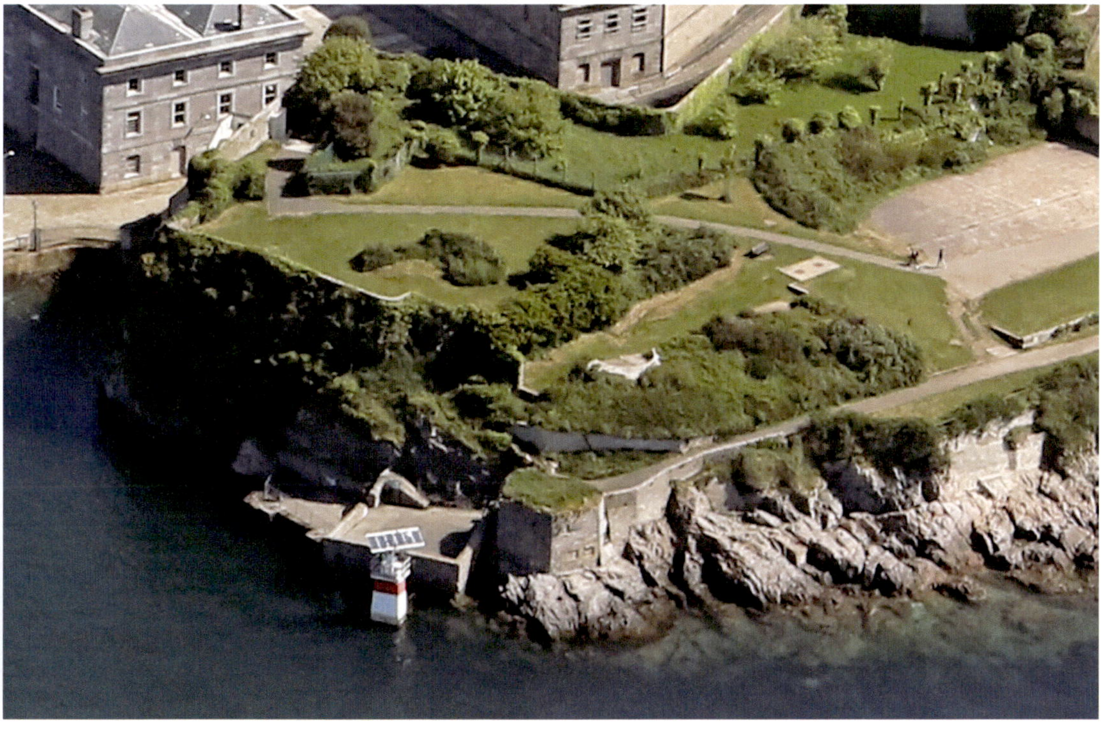

Devil's Point Battery.

Drake's Island

Three 12-pounder quick-firing guns were mounted by 1898 and remained throughout the First World War.

Eastern King

Between 1900 and 1912 four 12-pounder quick-firing guns had been mounted as anti-torpedo boat defence. Reduced to two by 1918.

Hawkins

In 1916 the redoubt is listed as mounting two 9.2-inch breech-loading high-angle guns. Manned by three officers and ninety-six other ranks.

Mount Wise

Still used as accommodation. Thirty-eight men from 10th Company Royal Engineers were shown living there in the 1911 census.

Penlee

During the First World War the three 9.2-inch guns remained in service, but one was removed in 1920.

Picklecombe

In 1914–18 the fort was manned by fifteen members of the Devon Royal Garrison Artillery (or RGA) (TA), with only the master gunner having his family with him. The 6-inch guns were used as the Examination Battery.

Pier Cellars

The nearby battery for two 12-pounder quick-firing guns which had been added by 1898 were dismounted by 1908 but were remounted during the First World War. Two searchlights were used to provide crossbeams to range the guns at night. The station was operated by a detachment of five members of the Royal Engineers, as listed in the census of 1911.

Polhawn

During the First World War the battery was used as officers' accommodation for Whitsand Bay Battery.

Rame

The old 9-inch guns had been replaced by 9.2-inch breech loaders on high-angle mounts. These were in place during the First World War.

Stamford

Used as barracks. In the 1911 census eighty men of the RGA were living there.

Tregantle

Also used as barracks. The 1911 census shows twenty-seven members of the Somerset Light Infantry, fifteen members of the Sherwood Foresters and thirty-three Royal Marine light infantrymen, plus an assortment of RE, RGA, Royal Army Service Corps and even one member of the 1st Leinster Regiment. It was virtually abandoned after the First World War.

Watchhouse

Reconstructed for two 6-inch breech loaders guns. Completed by 1903 and remained armed during the First World War. Its purpose was to cover the seaward approaches to the Sound.

Western King

Listed in 1911 as having seven 12-pounder quick-firing guns, but by 1918 this had been reduced to four.

Whitsand Bay Battery

Used during the First World War as soldiers' accommodation.

One establishment that few may have heard of appeared early in the First World War, and that was Royal Naval Air Station Laira. Established as a subsidiary of Royal Naval Air Station *Mullion* on the Lizard in Cornwall, the Royal Naval Air Service took over the old racecourse at Chelson Meadow, owned by Lord Morley of Saltram House. Now lost under several thousands of tons of rubbish after many years of being used as a council waste tip, Chelson Meadow was a flat area of reclaimed ground – ideal for horse racing. Its proximity to the Laira inlet made it an ideal place to moor and operate dirigible airships. It was home to two SSZ (Sea Scout Zero) airships, used to escort convoys and keep watch for German U-boats in the Western Approaches.

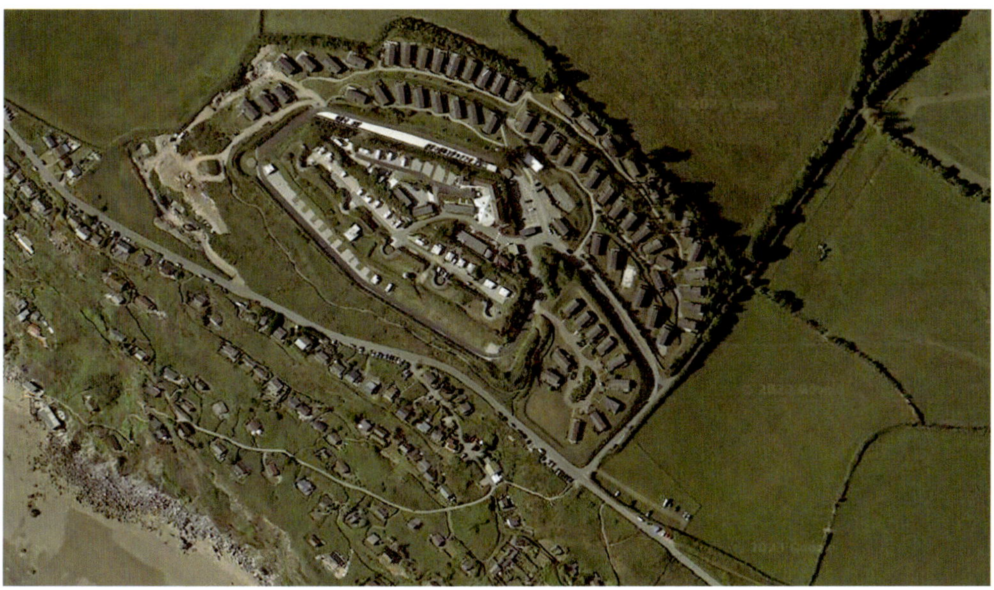

Whitsand Bay Battery, now a holiday park.

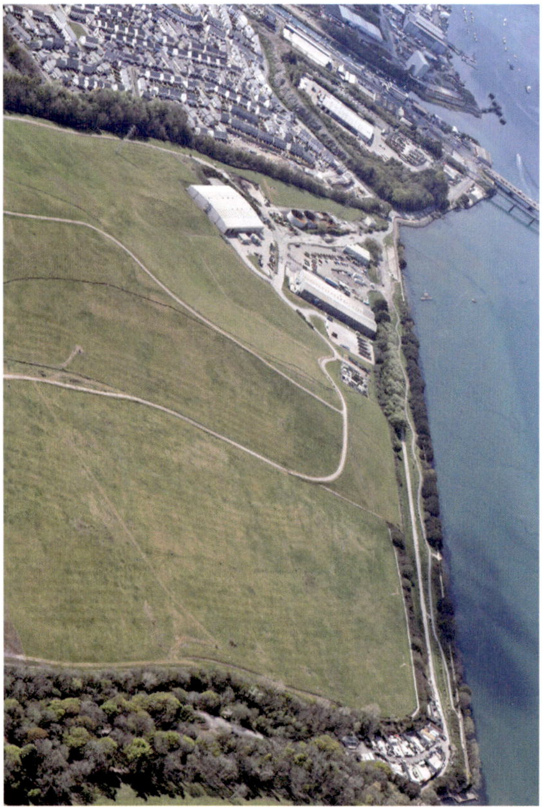

Chelson Meadow, site of RNAS Laira.

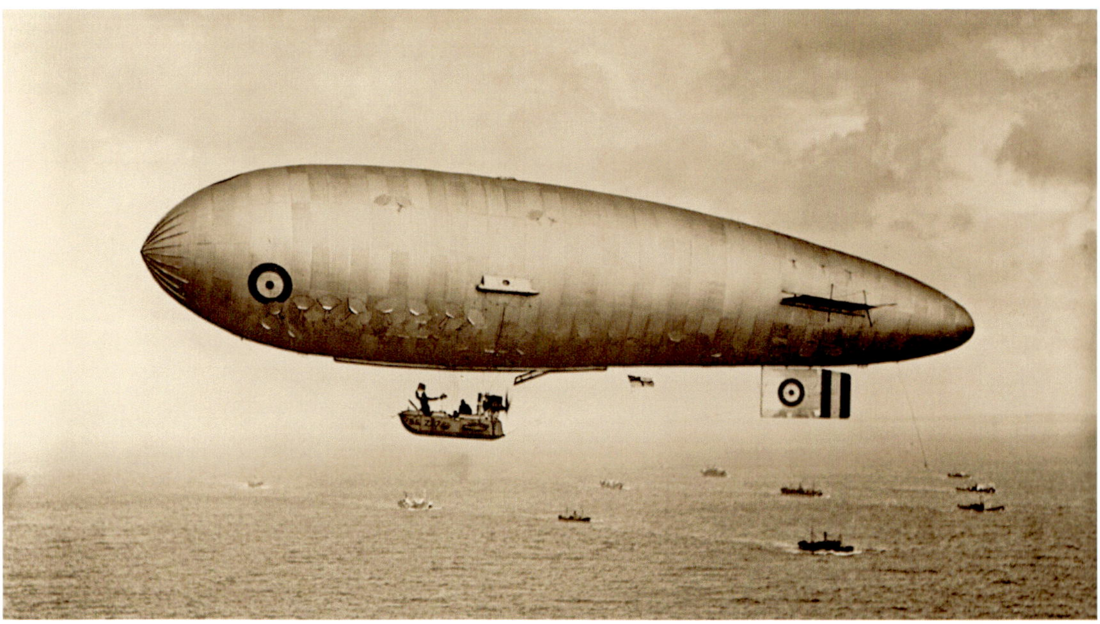

SSZ Class airship as based at RNAS Laira. (Imperial War Museums)

According to Brian Mosely's Old Plymouth website:

> Eye-witnesses said they were moored to the trees and painted in a camouflage khaki, brown and black. The ground crew of around twenty men slept on the wooden benches in the open-fronted race-course grandstand.

It was apparently still in use at the end of the war because in 1918 a visiting airship from Mullion crashed into the River Plym, having lost control in high winds. After the war the racetrack continued to be used as a landing ground by civilian pilots. Given the fact that there are so few areas of level ground around Plymouth, I can understand the popularity of this flat piece of ground.

Just down the River Plym another RNAS base was set up in 1917, but this one was for seaplanes. This was RNAS *Cattewater*. Two hangers were erected and a railway track was laid along the length of the pre-existing Mount Batten Pier (built in 1881) to enable a mobile steam crane to move along it, lifting the Short 184 seaplanes into and out of the water.

On 1 April 1918 the Royal Naval Air Service was merged with the Royal Flying Corps to become the Royal Air Force and the station was re-commissioned as Royal Air Force Cattewater, then from 1928 it was known as RAF Mount Batten. At last Plymouth now had representatives of all the services in the area, with the Royal Navy in barracks at HMS *Drake* as well as the ships in the dockyard, the Royal Marines in Stonehouse Barracks, the army in the various forts and barracks around the city, plus of course the Royal Citadel and now the brand-new service, the Royal Air Force.

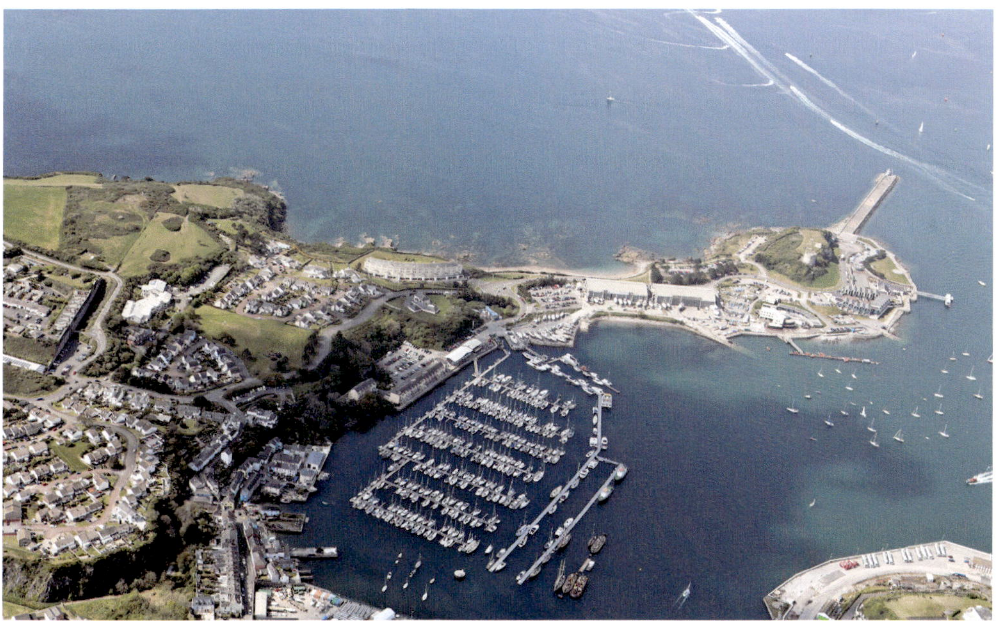

Mount Batten, site of RNAS Cattewater.

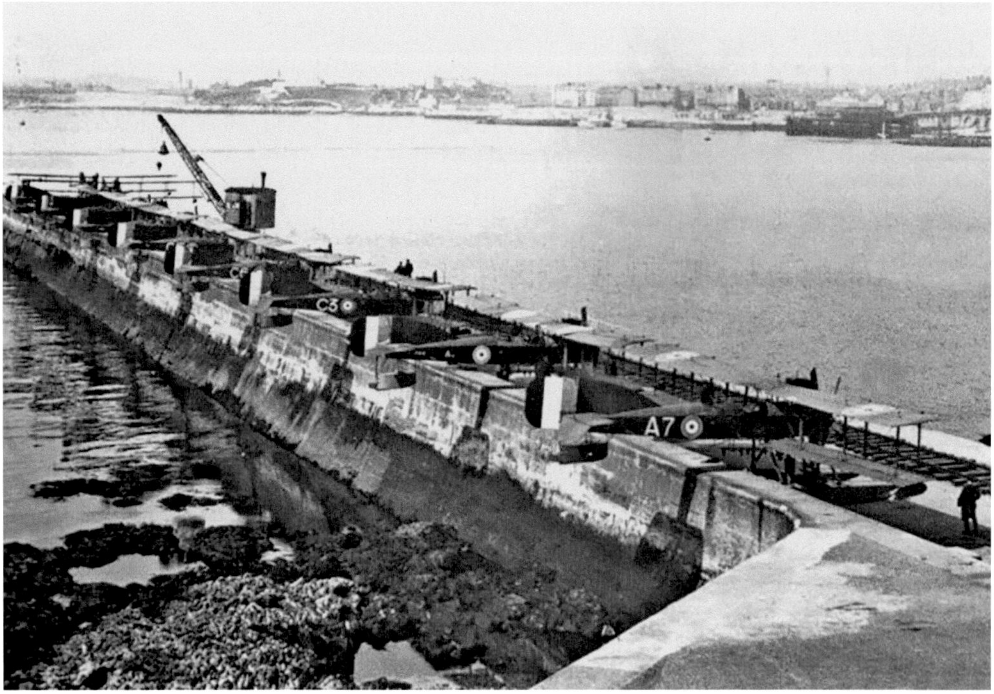

Short 184s lined up along Mount Batten Pier. (Courtesy of britishempire.co.uk)

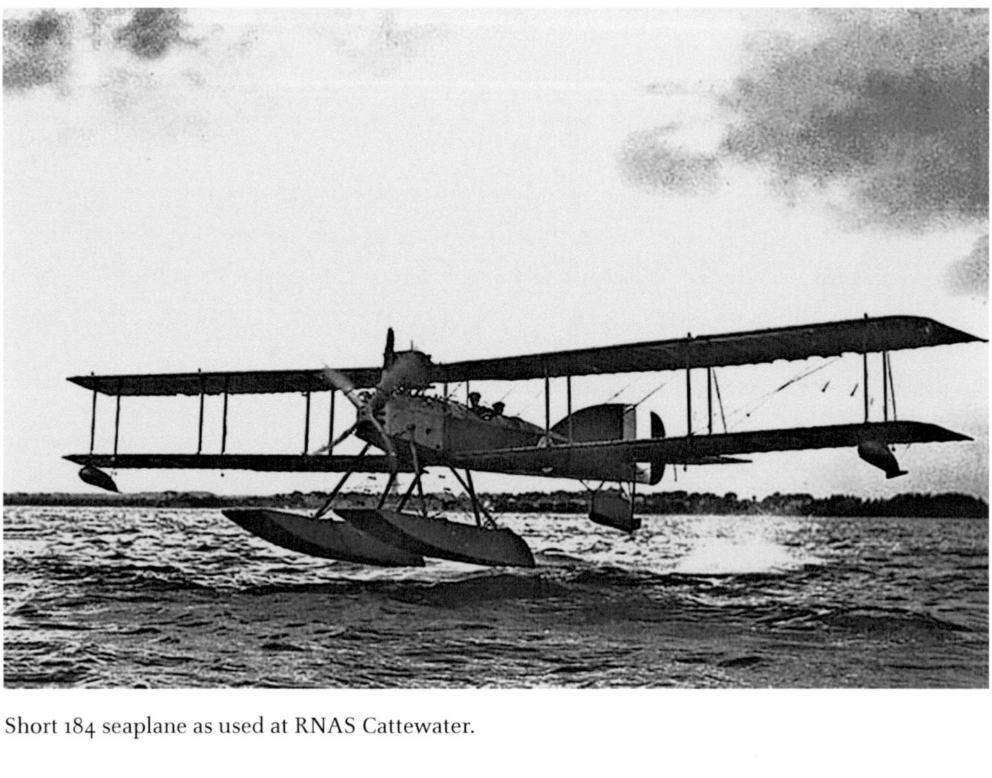

Short 184 seaplane as used at RNAS Cattewater.

The Interwar Years

In 1933 the need for an access road from the Barbican to the Hoe meant cutting through the Lower Fort, the walls joining the Citadel to the now obsolete Fisher's Nose Battery. Prior to this there was only pedestrian access through a gated tunnel known as the Cage Walk. This gave us Madeira Road which winds around the seafront.

Another place that later became part of the Royal Air Force was the polo field beside the Tavistock Road, near the George Hotel. This was first used as a temporary airstrip by Alan Cobham on 28 September 1923 and continued in operation for a month, flying proving flights which were intended to carry mail, parcels and passengers to cities around the country. In 1929 the Air Ministry acquired the site and Royal Engineers from the Plymouth garrison turned the polo field and two fields adjoining into an aerodrome. The site was only required for a couple of days each week during June, July and August 1929, and at the time they had no intention of making it a permanent airfield. According to royalnavyresearcharchive.org.uk:

> [The] site was licensed as an aerodrome in 1930; it was also chosen to become a civic airport and Plymouth City Council bought the site at Roborough for £20,478. After further development the aerodrome was officially opened by HRH the Prince of Wales on July 15th 1931. The site had four small hangars, and during the 1930s was used by the Plymouth & District Aero Club, and Great Western Railway, Railway Air Services, Channel Air Ferries and the Great Western & Southern Air Lines and Jersey Airways. One of the hangars was unique in that its design had the control tower on top of the roof.

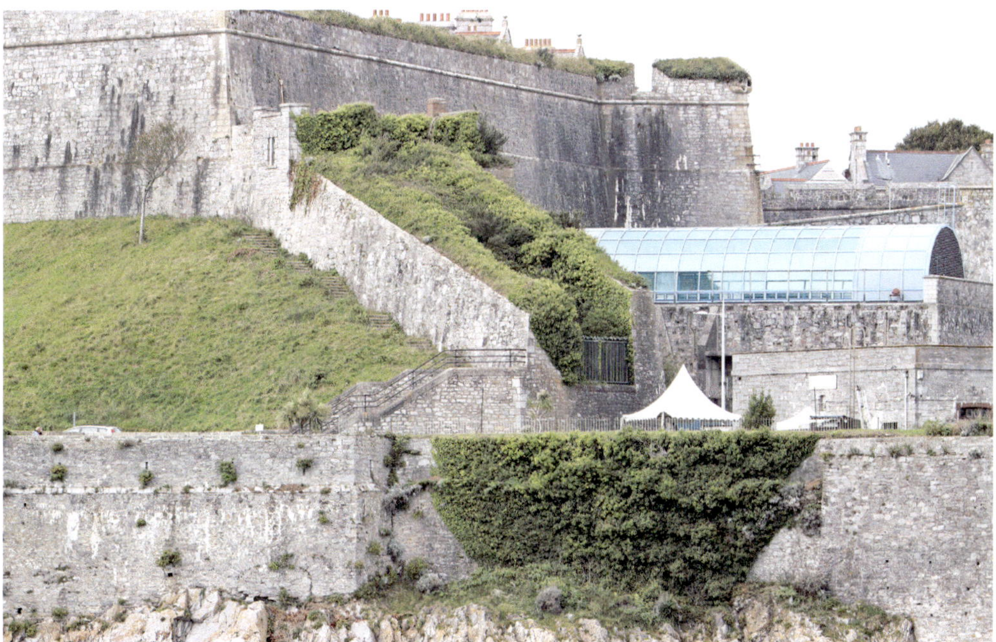

Truncated Lower Fort walls to allow the passage of Madeira Road.

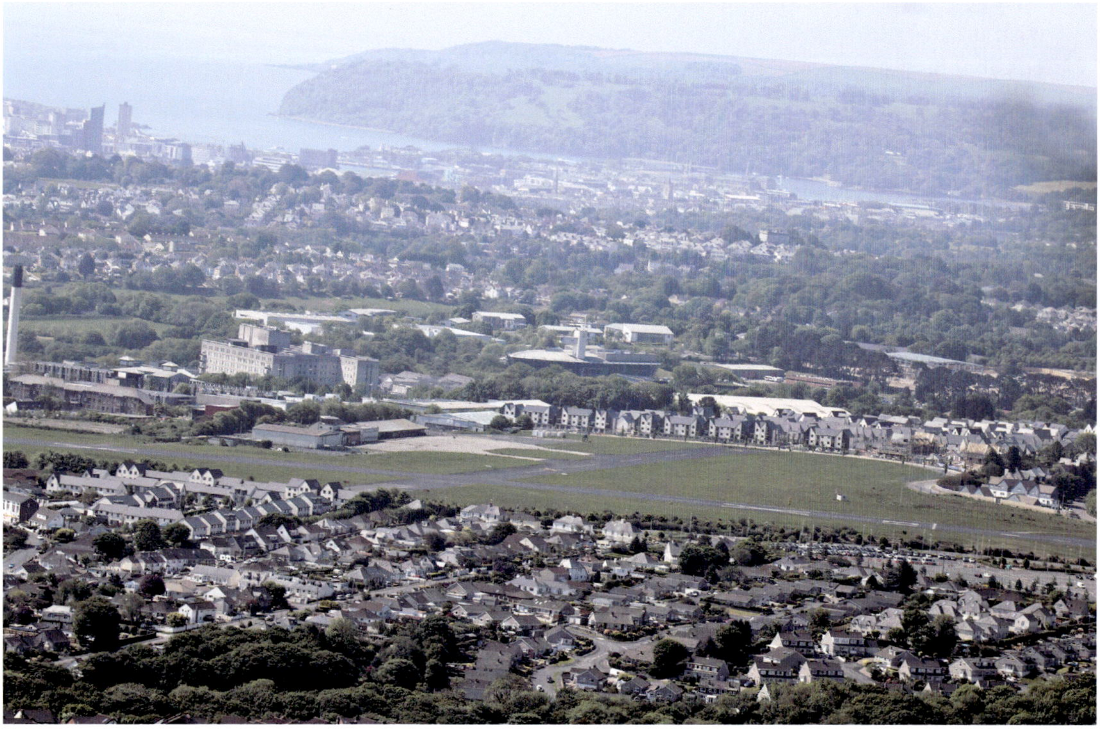

Roborough airfield today.

Having once had an aircraft based at Roborough, what is obvious to me is that all the people who used to complain about the aircraft noise must have moved into houses beside an existing airfield, because few could have been there since before 1930. Did they not expect aircraft noise living next to an established airfield?

The Second World War

Although the Royal Navy's Fleet Air Arm, the later incarnation of the old Royal Naval Air Service, had used Roborough occasionally from 1937 onwards, mainly for inter-service co-operation exercises, the aerodrome was requisitioned by the Admiralty shortly after the declaration of war with Germany and opened as RN Air Station Roborough. The station was used mainly for embarking and disembarking aircraft to and from aircraft carriers up to June 1940.

From August 1940 only RAF units operated from the station. The fairly short runway meant it was restricted to use by smaller aircraft, mainly Gloster Gladiator II biplanes and Hawker Hurricanes tasked with the defence of the south-west of England, including the ports of Plymouth and Falmouth. There were also visits from the occasional Supermarine Walrus and Westland Lysanders. Having been initially requisitioned by the Admiralty, during 1942 ownership passed to the Air Ministry, making it an official RAF base.

The next place to appear was RAF Harrowbeer, near Yelverton. Much of this information came from the RAF Harrowbeer website. Construction started in late 1940, with the airfield officially opening on 15 August 1941, although some think there might possibly have been a grass airfield on the site previously. It was a fighter station and, like Roborough, the runways were not long enough for heavy bombers and the south-west is too far from those bombers' destinations. It was under the control of 10 Group Fighter Command, which was responsible for the defence of the south-west of England. Many different nationalities flew from Harrowbeer, mostly RAF squadrons, including Polish and Czech pilots, but also Fleet Air Arm and US Navy.

Although near the village of Yelverton, the airfield was called Harrowbeer to distinguish it from the similar-sounding RNAS Yeovilton in Somerset. It was built with three Tarmac runways in the classic RAF 'A' shape. On 21 October 1941 No. 276 Air Sea Rescue Squadron was formed within Knightstone House, which was also their headquarters until February 1943 when they transferred across the road to Ravenscroft.

RAF Harrowbeer's immediate role was to protect shipping in the English Channel between Land's End, Cornwall, and Weymouth, Dorset. Their primary objective was to offer protection against the German U-boats and E-boats, although by early 1942 the squadrons also undertook the escort of bombers to France and back. On 10 October 1942 No. 175 Squadron arrived with their Hurricane fighter/bomber aircraft, which were to carry out low-level shipping strikes.

No. 193 Squadron was formed at RAF Harrowbeer on 18 December 1942. It took delivery of four Hurricane and three Typhoon aircraft on 14 January 1943. After local familiarisation flights, they assisted Nos 263 and 266 squadrons with bombing attacks on railways and airfields in France.

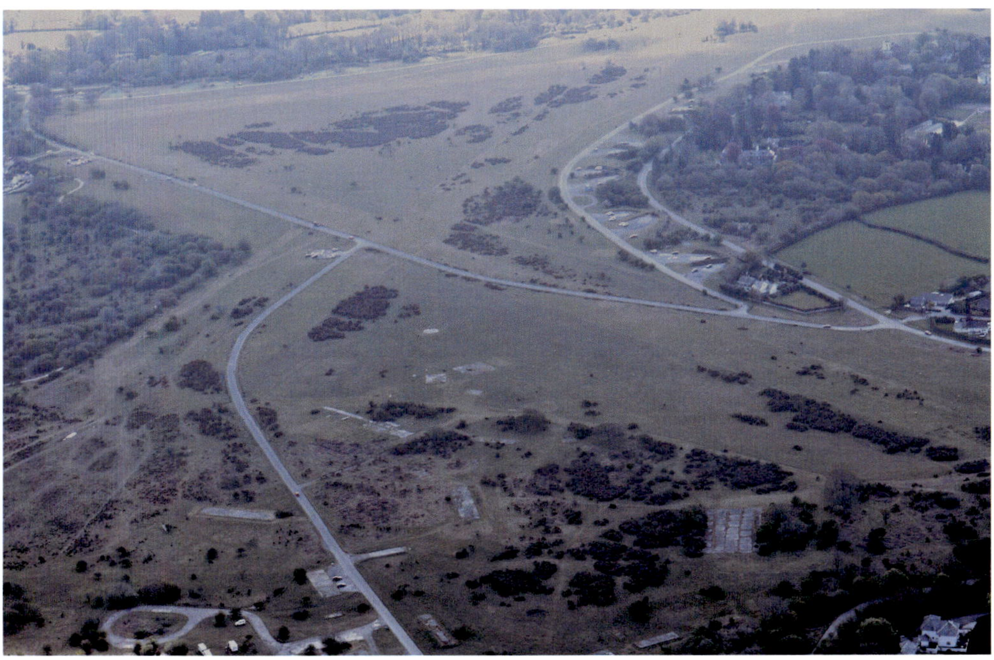

Harrowbeer with the runways still just visible.

The Typhoon was never much loved; the Napier-Sabre 24-cylinder sleeve-valve engine was unreliable and difficult to start in cold weather and there were instances of the tails coming off the aircraft in flight when pulling out of a high-speed dive. At one time, more pilots had been killed by these failures than by enemy action.

From early 1944 RAF Harrowbeer's Typhoon aircraft were converted to carry rocket projectiles and used for concentrated attacks on shipping, radar and communication sites in France. There is a report of a heavily loaded Typhoon clipping the Yelverton Church tower after take-off from Harrowbeer. According to the WartimeNI website:

> Jack Pringle, Belfast-born airman died at Harrowbeer, Yelverton, Devon at 1155hrs on 28th May 1944 aged 21 years old. He was the pilot of Hawker Typhoon EK211 with RAF 263 Squadron. On an air-to-air firing and dive-bombing practice, the plane hit the tower of St. Paul's Church.

The pilot died in the accident, but despite falling masonry the vicar continued with the morning service. Apparently after this accident the red light on the tower was replaced by a black and white board to increase visibility.

On 31 August 1944 RAF Harrowbeer was closed as an RAF station and taken over by the USAAF. However, on 8 January 1945 the airfield was back in the hands of the RAF until being placed on 'Care and Maintenance' on 31 July 1945. It finally closed in 1950 and the runways were torn up during the 1960s.

The previously mentioned RAF Mount Batten continued to be used as a seaplane station right through the war with RAF and RAAF aircraft, including the famous Sunderland flying boats, operating against U-boats in the battle. Given the awful weather we sometimes get in Plymouth, it is perhaps a surprise to find that there were few accidents and crashes. Some aircraft were damaged after slipping their moorings in strong winds and ending up on the rocks and a few aircraft failed to take off. One, which Dennis Teague mentioned in his book about the station, crashed and sank, at which point the anti-submarine depth charges exploded and killed both the aircrew and the boat crew who had come to rescue them.

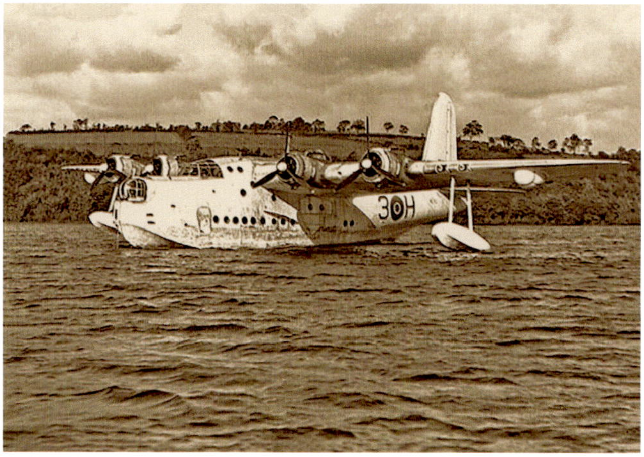

Short Sunderland as flown from RAF Mount Batten.

One aircraft that did crash was Short Sunderland Mk II W6054, on 13 November 1942, having flown up from Gibraltar in appalling weather (which apparently the forecasters had not foreseen – nothing changes!). Eventually the navigator decided they must be near Plymouth, but the fog was so thick the pilot could not even see the sea. Running low on fuel, he decided to attempt a blind landing. The aircraft hit the water at cruising speed with the altimeter still reading 600 feet. The impact destroyed the aircraft, but all the crew survived, though sadly none of the passengers did. We know all this because in the 1980s diver Neil Griffin found and salvaged the aircraft's propeller. It is now on display at the RAAF's Association Museum at Bull Creek near Perth.

As a child living in Cawsand in the 1950s, I recall seeing a Sunderland taking off from the Sound. The last flight was in 1959 according to the Old Plymouth website.

Mount Wise MHQ

In 1942, as part of the planning for D-day, there was a requirement for 'protected tactical communications facilities'. This resulted in the digging of a series of tunnels in the south-western corner of Mount Wise which were finished by early 1944. They were connected to all the HQs as well as the local services. After the war the bunker became HQ CinC Plymouth. In 1951 it became the Maritime HQ or MHQ. It was used as a high-tech communications centre for joint-service liaison and organisation for intelligence, exercises and operations. It remained in service use until 2004.

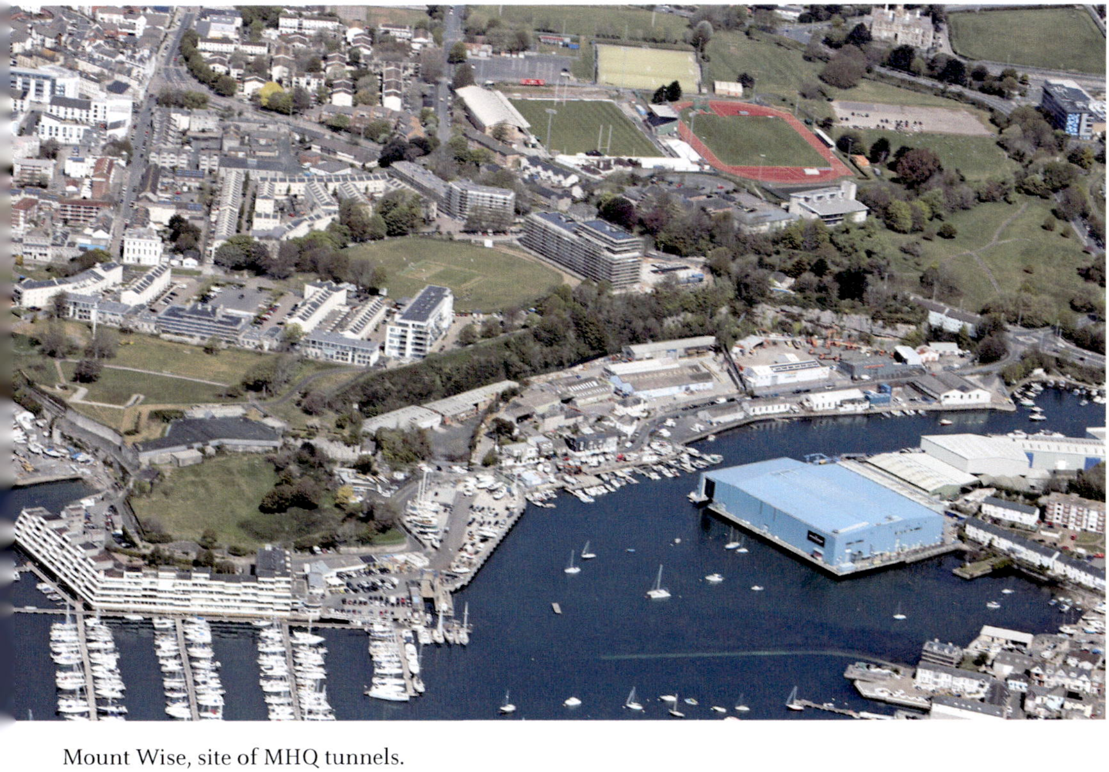

Mount Wise, site of MHQ tunnels.

Anti-Aircraft Measures

As air attacks increased, 3.7-inch heavy anti-aircraft batteries and radar towers were installed around Plymouth. As I have said previously, exact data about what went on in wartime is hard to find. Much of this information came from the RA39-45 website.

Billacombe

Located beside the quarry with six six 3.7-inch static guns.

Wembury Point

Six 3.7-inch static guns.

Home Park

Opposite Seagrave Road with four 3.7-inch static guns.

Hooe Hill

Z4 anti-aircraft rocket battery with sixty-four projectors as recalled in a Youtube video by David Hoskin who served there during the Second World War.

Maker Barracks

Six 3.7-inch static guns by 1942.

Maker

In the field in front of the church. Z3 anti-aircraft rocket battery. Sixty U2P and four UP projectors.

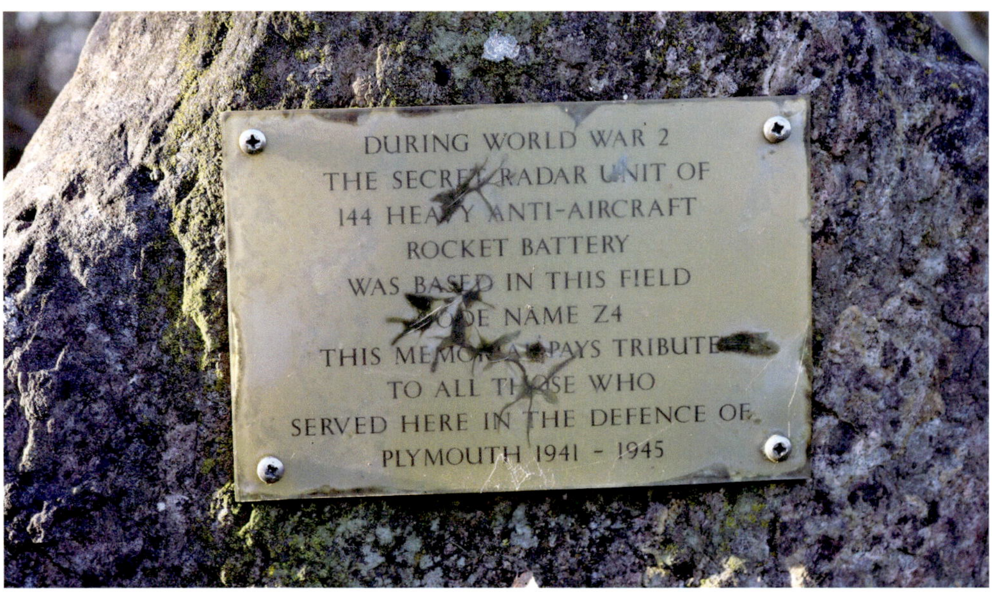

Plaque showing position of radar unit for Z4 battery at Hooe Hill.

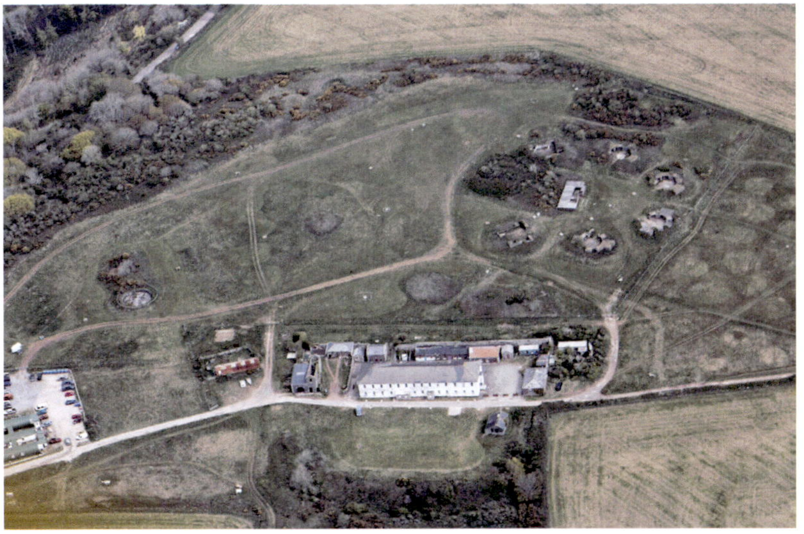

Maker Barracks with Second World War AA site behind.

Pier Cellars

The site was used during the Second World War as a Harbour Defence (ASDIC) Station.

Rame

Penlee, left of road. Six 3.7-inch static guns by 1942.

Rame

Chain Home Low 15a antenna (opposite Rame Church).

Rame Head

Chain Home Low K167 antenna near Rame Head Chapel.

Seaton Barracks, Crownhill

Four 3.7-inch static guns (later six).

Torpoint

Near Horson Cemetery. Six 3.7-inch mobile guns by 1942.

Higher Tregantle

Between Higher Tregantle Farm and the Engineered Foam Products factory. Four 3.7-inch static guns.

Barrage Balloons

Barrage balloons were rigged at numerous locations, including Staddon Heights and Devonport Park. Apparently, the copper ball on the top of the Naval War Memorial on the Hoe has a dent in it, which was caused by being hit by the shackle of a runaway barrage balloon which ended up draped over the Strathmore Hotel.

To counter the E-boat (fast torpedo boats) threat, many of the Victorian waterside defences were upgraded, although the focus was installation of searchlights and quick-firing guns. Mount Batten, Drake's Island, Eastern and Western King Batteries, Devil's Point, Fort Bovisand and Fort Picklecombe all had coastal defence batteries installed, whilst anti-aircraft batteries were placed in many of the forts – their deep and large magazines making them ideally suited for this purpose.

Wartime Use of the Palmerston Forts

Austin

During the Second World War the fort was occupied by the Devon and Cornwall Auxiliary Unit. These auxiliary units were the men who had been trained in guerilla tactics and usually given a hidden bolthole from which they could launch attacks on the German forces if Britain had been invaded. This had seemed possible, maybe even likely, after Dunkirk. They were known as 'the Stay Behinds' because they would stay and fight the invaders when everyone else would flee to safety. Thankfully they were never needed.

J. S. W. Edmundson, from the South West Area (Devon and Cornwall) Intelligence Office, initially made use of Fort Austin in Plymouth as a store and headquarters between July 1940 and September 1943 according to staybehinds.com.

Bovisand

Other than the practice battery and the 12-pounder battery at nearby Staddon Point, the fort remained unarmed until the Second World War when two twin 6-pounder quick-firing guns where emplaced together with their directing towers on the roof, with Casemates 11 and 16 being converted into magazines.

Breakwater

In 1936 it became an Anti-Aircraft Training School with additional AA guns and used as a lookout and signalling station.

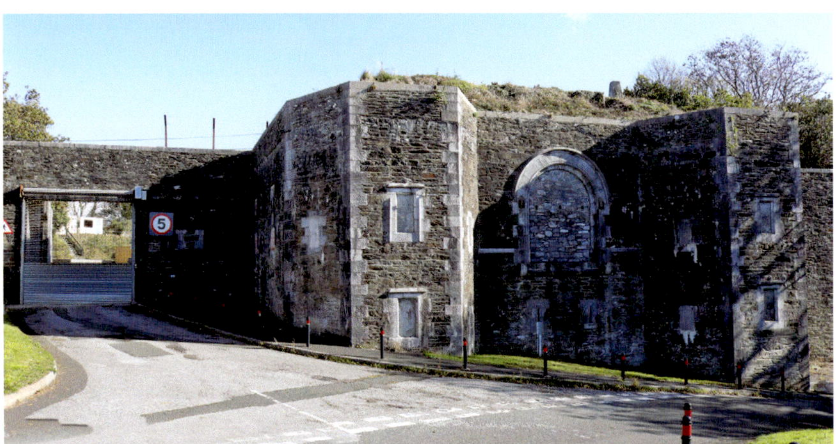

Fort Austin entrance, HQ of the Stay-behinds.

Crownhill

After the First World War it was first a de-mobilisation depot. After that it was a base for the then new Royal Corps of Signals, a barrack for the 2nd Battalion the Royal Devonshire Regiment, then, after Dunkirk, it was converted into a strong point in the 'Plymouth Outer Ring Defences'.

Plumer Barracks

The new name for the 1891 Crownhill Barracks, across Tavistock Road from the fort, were used to accommodate American forces during the Second World War.

Seaton Barracks

The new name for the Crownhill Hutments, slightly further out along Tavistock Road, was used as an AA site during the Second World War. Pictures show six emplacements.

Devil's Point

In 1918 one gun remained and in 1941 the battery buildings were used by troops manning the boom defence. The two gun emplacements are still visible.

Drake's Island

In 1942 it had two twin 6-pounder and two 12-pounder guns. All emplacements survive intact.

Eastern King

In 1940 there was one 40-mm Bofors and an observation post.

Ernesettle

It was used in the Second World War as part of the General Line of Defence for Plymouth, possibly as an anti-aircraft observation post and fire-watching post. It was used after this as Royal Naval stores and now stands inside the perimeter of the RN armament depot.

Garden Battery

I have seen unsubstantiated reports that during the Second World War it is possible that two light quick-firing guns were installed to defend the boom extending across to Devil's Point to match the gun there. Having been used during the First World War, it was disarmed after 1927 and abandoned by the Ministry of Defence in 1948.

Hawkins

Coast Battery was stood down in 1922 and re-occupied by the military in 1940. There is some indication that barrage balloon personnel used the fort from time to time during the war and it is therefore safe to assume that more than one military unit used the battery from 1939 to 1945. It was retained post-war and was finally relinquished in 1953, then sold in 1959.

Lentney

By 1941 one twin 6-pounder quick-firing gun was added with two 6-inch BL naval guns and two 12-pounder quick-firing guns – all for training purposes. During the Second World War Lentney served as the practice battery for the Coast Artillery training regiment based in Fort Staddon.

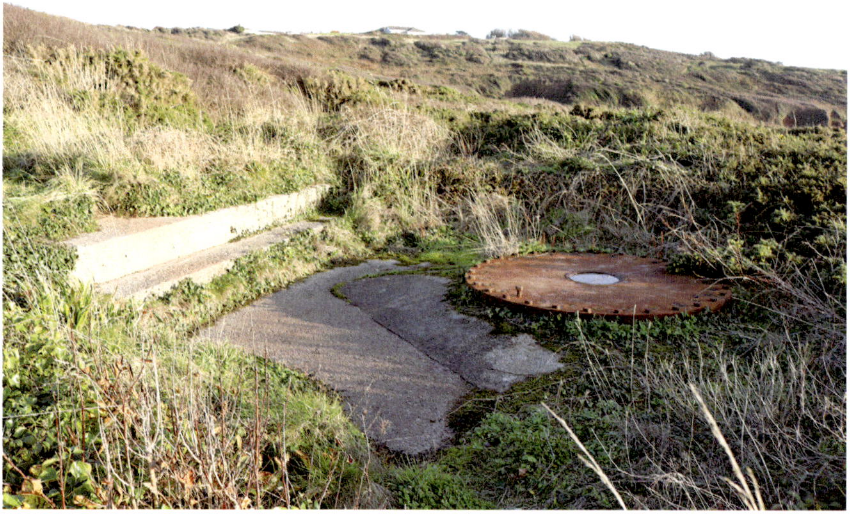

Lentney coastal battery with Lentney Battery on the hill behind.

A new emplacement for one twin 6-pounder gun was mounted for training in 1942 on the coast, approximately 200 m west of Lentney Battery.

Lord Howard

The First World War guns had been removed by 1936. Two guns were mounted again in 1941 and manned by troops from nearby Fort Stamford. In 1946 the battery was disarmed.

Penlee

Battery had three 9.2-inch guns manned by 164 Battery 567 Coast Regt RA. The guns were removed in 1956.

Picklecombe (Hooe Lake)

According to the RA 39-45 website there was one 3-inch gun at Hooe Lake, just down the coast to the west of Picklecombe Fort. I have also seen claims there were range finder and searchlight positions there as well.

Picklecombe Fort

During the Second World War the fort became active again as the Examination Battery and crews from 162 and 163 Batteries of the Devonshire heavy regiment, which became 567 Coast Regt RA, manned the forts armament of two 6-inch breech loaders and two 6-pounder quick firing whilst the RE manned the Defence Electric Lights and the navy worked the off-shore controlled minefield. In 1956 the fort was released by the military.

Pier Cellars

During the Second World War the station was used for the development and testing of one- and two-man torpedoes of the Welman Chariot type.

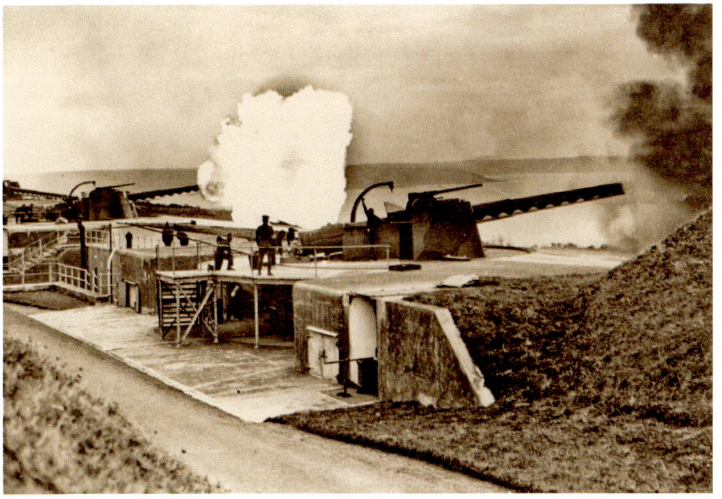

Penlee Battery with gun firing. (Courtesy of Steve Johnson, cyberheritage)

Renney Brake

Long-range 35° mountings for the three 9.2-inch guns were emplaced in the Second World War, increasing the range of the guns to 35,000 yards. In addition, the battery received two 60 pounders, one mobile 6-pounder gun and two 40 mm Bofors LAA guns.

Staddon Fort

Possibly used for searchlights during the Second World War.

Staddon Heights

Used as a battery office and store.

Staddon Point (Bovisand)

One 6-inch gun according to the RA 39-45 website. According to the Victorian Forts website 'emplacement No. 2 was altered first for a rocket launcher (projector) and then a 40mm LAA Bofors gun in 1943'.

Tregantle

It was abandoned after the First World War. On the outbreak of the Second World War it became the Army Gas School until 1942 when it was used as accommodation for the US Army. After 1945 it reverted to the British Army.

Western King

Below the 12-pounder quick-firing battery of the First World War, two emplacements for twin 6-pounder quick-firing guns were added in 1941. The guns were dismounted in 1956.

Watch House

Armed with 6-inch breech loaders guns during the First World War, the guns remained through the Second World War. They were stood down in 1946 and dismounted in 1956.

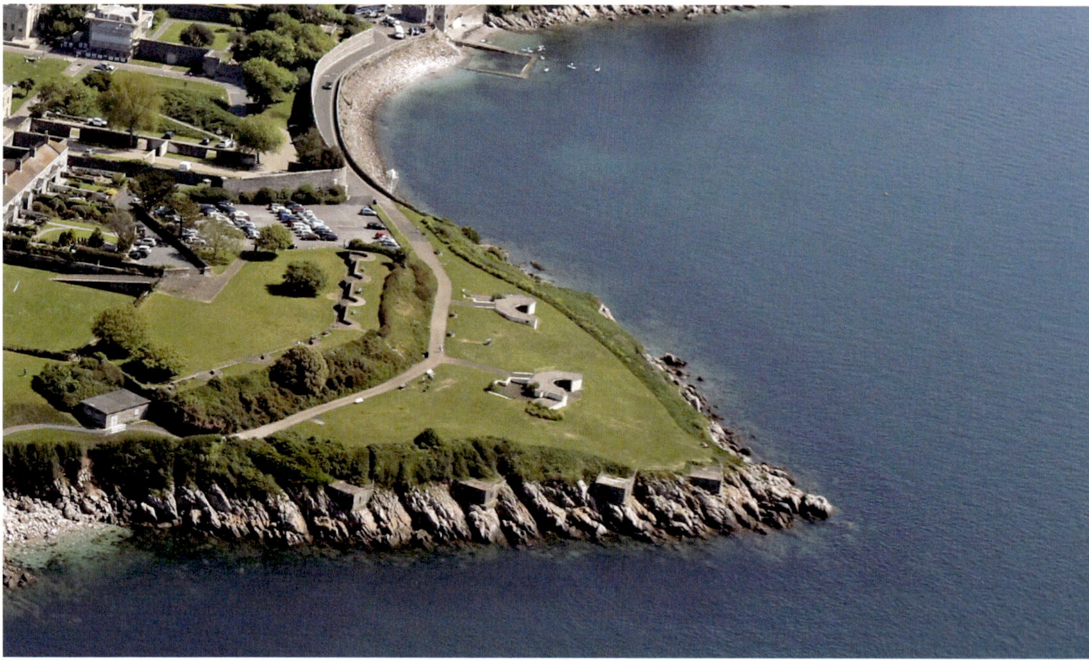

Old Western King Redoubt with Second World War gun sites in front.

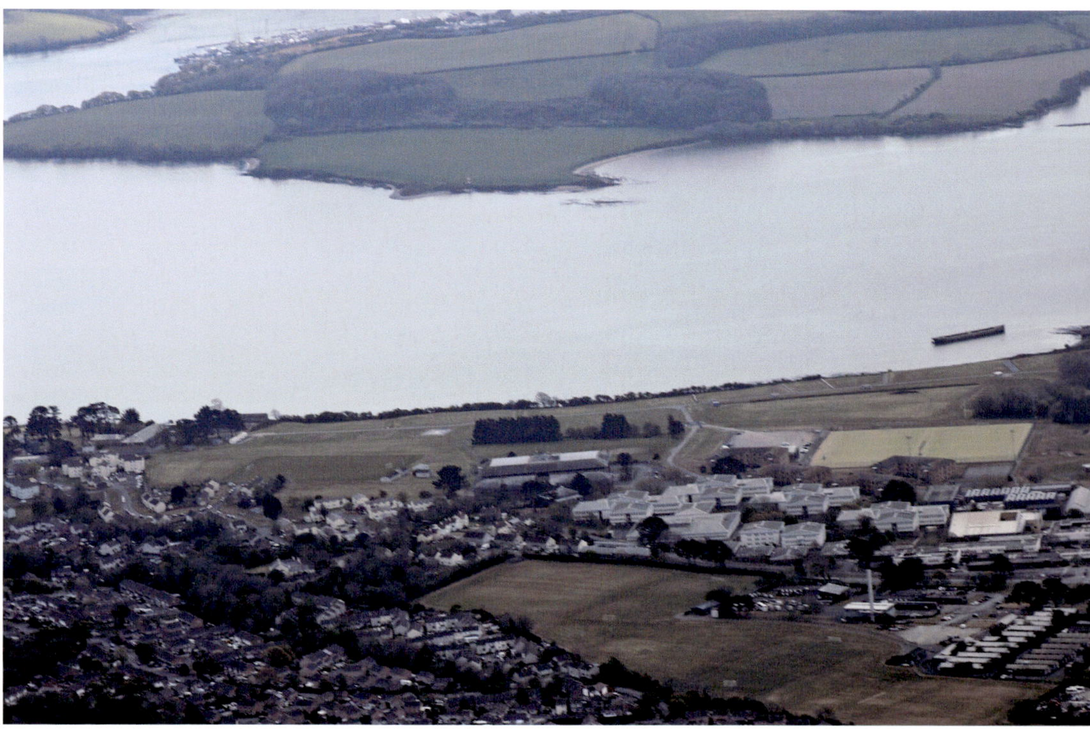

HMS *Raleigh* at Torpoint.

Bickleigh Barracks

Built by A. F. French & Co. in early 1940 and reportedly originally designated as a sewage disposal farm, but Plymouth needed an evacuee camp though the first occupants were Free French and Polish servicemen. By 1942 it was returned to the Civil Defence Organisation for its original purpose of housing refugees. The camp was called the General Evacuation Centre (South West).

HMS *Raleigh*

Commissioned in January 1940 as a training establishment to train the men conscripted for wartime military service.

HMS *Cambridge*

There had been a naval gunnery school locally since 1856, originally based aboard an eighty-gun third rate called HMS *Cambridge*. As was the way of things with training ships, when the original ship was scrapped it would be replaced with another ship but the name was retained. The gunnery school was moved onto land at the Plymouth naval barracks in 1907 where it remained until 1940 when the old Wembury Point Holiday Camp was taken over as a gunnery range used by both the army and navy.

Turnchapel

Turnchapel had a history of shipbuilding and repairing since the seventeenth century. The site was used by the Admiralty as a naval oil fuel depot from 1903, but the tanks were destroyed during the Blitz in 1940. The Americans used the slipway as an embarkation point during the Normandy landings in June 1944.

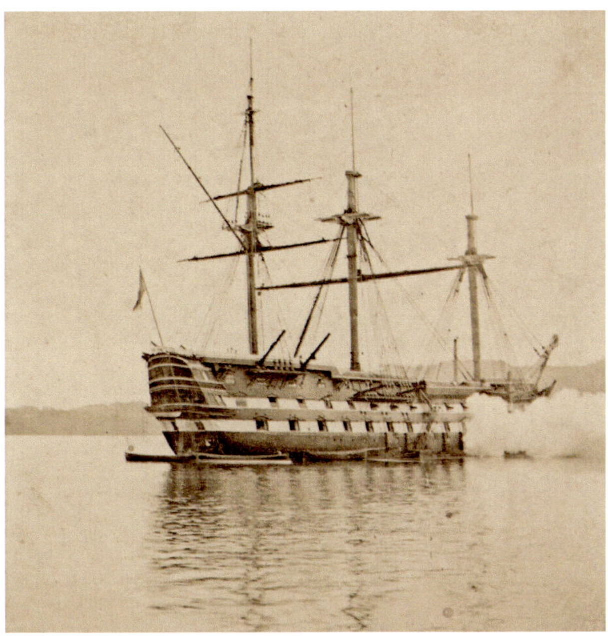

HMS *Cambridge* in Hamoaze, 1869. (Courtesy of Rijksmuseum, CC0 1.0)

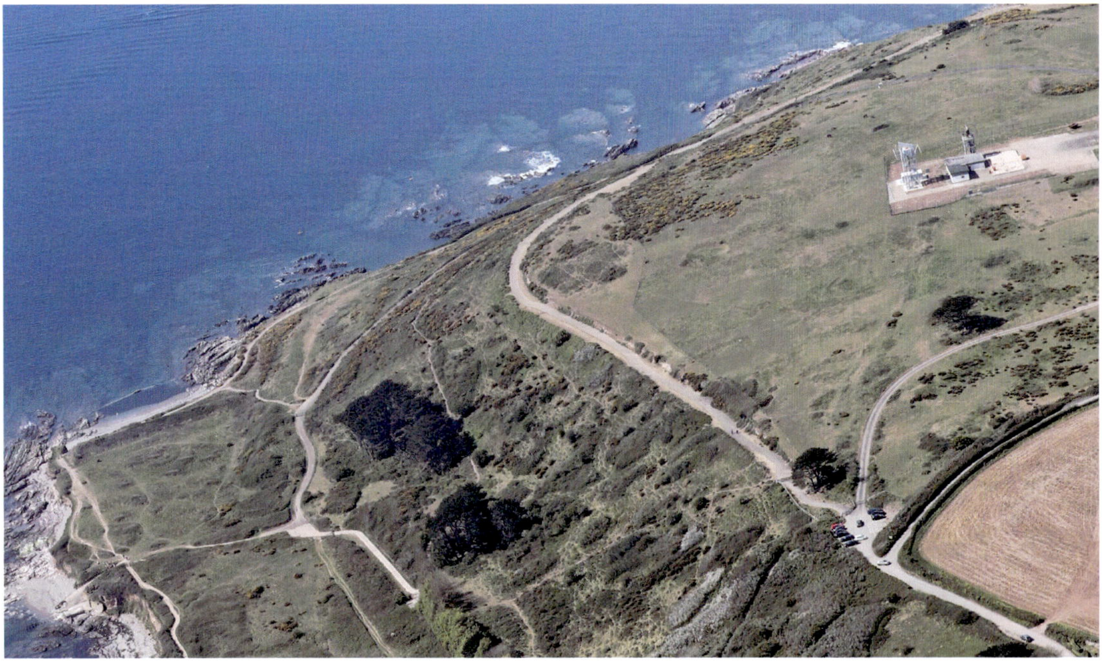

HMS *Cambridge* site with radar station still operating.

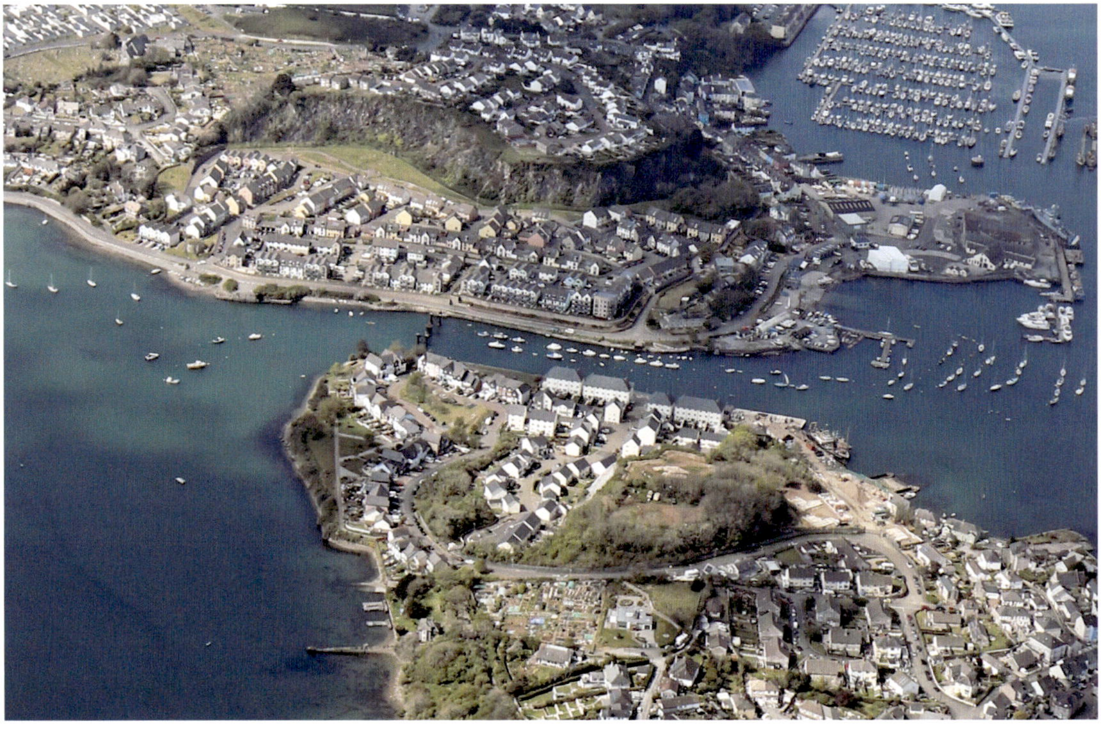

Turnchapel.

7. Up to the Present Day

Between the end of the Second World War and the present day there has been a massive run down of the armed forces. According to the Statista website, the peak number of serving forces personnel was 4.69 million in 1945; in 2022 there were 147,980, with a commensurate reduction in ships, aircraft, tanks, etc. With fewer naval ships came a reduction in the size of the dockyard. In its heyday in 1945, some 20,000 people worked in Devonport Dockyard; today, if Wikipedia is to be believed, it employs just 2,500. Most of the original dockyard area in South Yard is now in civilian hands.

Because of this massive reduction in the size of the armed forces, there has also been a massive reduction in requirements for facilities. Many have been repurposed, some have found new uses with civilian owners and some are simply abandoned.

Roborough Airport

It returned to civilian use after the war, although in 1961 the Britannia Royal Naval College Air Experience Flight was formed at Roborough to provide flying experience for Dartmouth officer cadets. In January 2007 this squadron moved to RNAS Yeovilton ending the Fleet Air Arm's long association with Roborough. Today the airport is closed thanks to Plymouth City Council.

Palmerston Forts

Of the Palmerston forts only a very few remained in armed forces use beyond the 1950s. Crownhill Fort had an active military role until the 1980s. Of the others, Eastern King remains under MoD control and is a Scheduled Monument. Pier Cellars remains in MoD navy use. Staddon Fort is currently used by the navy for communications, with masts sited on the parade. Scraesdon and Tregantle are both under military control. Ernesettle Fort is still in the care of the MoD, being in the grounds of RNAD Ernesettle, but it is not used for anything. RNAD Bullpoint is now used for emergency disaster training.

Bickleigh Barracks

By the end of the war Polish naval personnel once again occupied the camp, but it was empty when the first Royal Marines, part of RM Training Group Devon, arrived on 1 April 1946 as an Infantry Training School. Later it became simply the Commando School RM until 1960. In 1971 the barracks became the home of 42 Commando, who remain there today.

HMS *Raleigh*

From 1950 onwards it became the RN centre for training mechanics. It is now the initial training centre for all RN recruits. It uses Pier Cellars as an assault course and

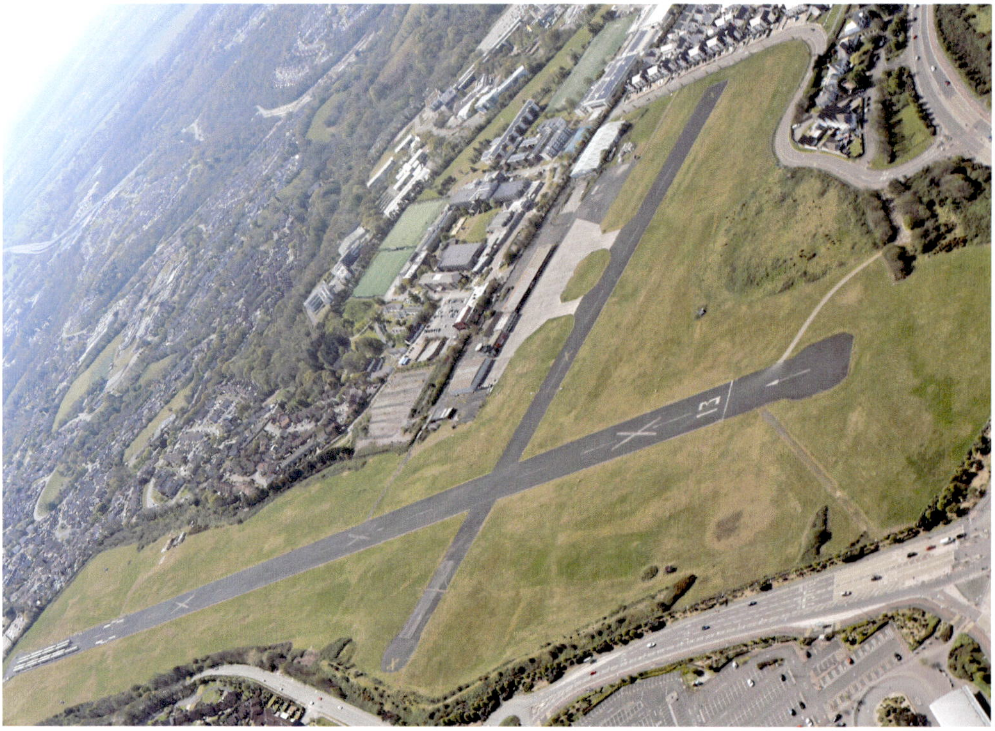

Roborough Airport closed.

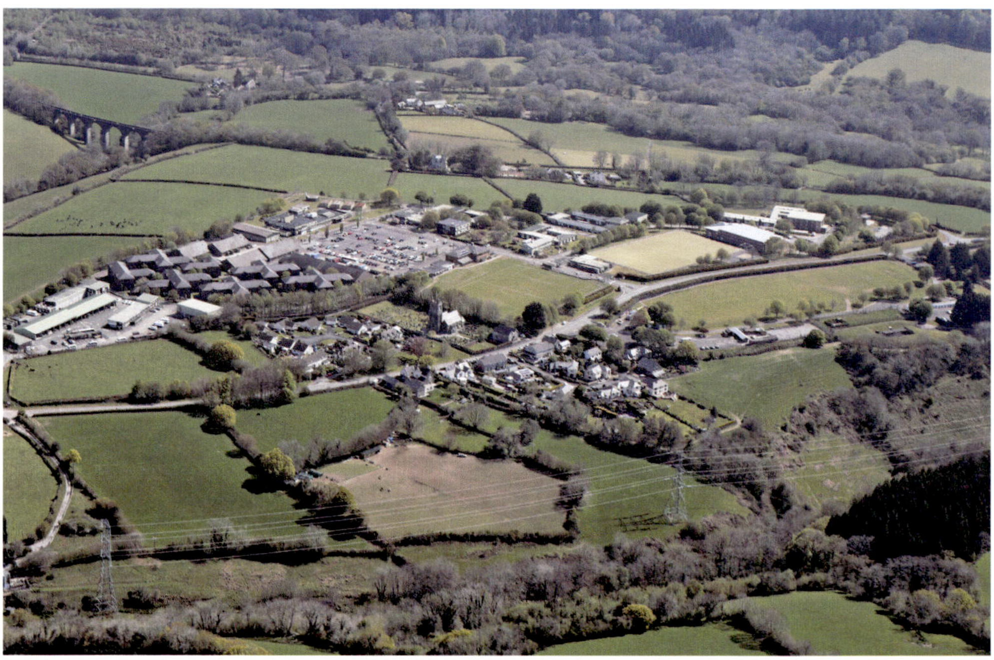

Bickleigh Barracks.

training base, and Jupiter Point with its static HMS *Brecon* for boat-handling experience. Jupiter Point is the site of the old HMS *Defiance*, on the Lynher between Antony estate and Wearde.

RM Barracks Stonehouse

The spiritual home of the Royal Marines and the Royal Citadel, home to 29 Commando Regiment, Royal Artillery, have both been under threat of closure for many years. At time of writing they are still in service.

Of those Palmerston forts not under military control, several have found good uses in civilian life: Hawkins Battery on Maker and Whitsand Bay Battery are now caravan sites. Agaton Fort is home to the Goods Vehicle Testing Station. Bowden Battery is now a garden centre. Cawsand Fort and Picklecombe Fort have both been converted for residential use. Crownhill Fort is now managed by the Landmark Trust, providing holiday accommodation and regular open days explaining the history of the fort. Drake's Island was run as an adventure training facility until 1989. It is now being converted to include a luxury hotel and education centre. Efford Fort is used as winter quarters for showmen. Eggbuckland Keep is being restored as a community project. Fort Austin is a Plymouth City Council depot. In 1984 the guardhouse was converted into the Plymouth City Emergency Centre for Civil Defence. Fort Bovisand is being converted for residential

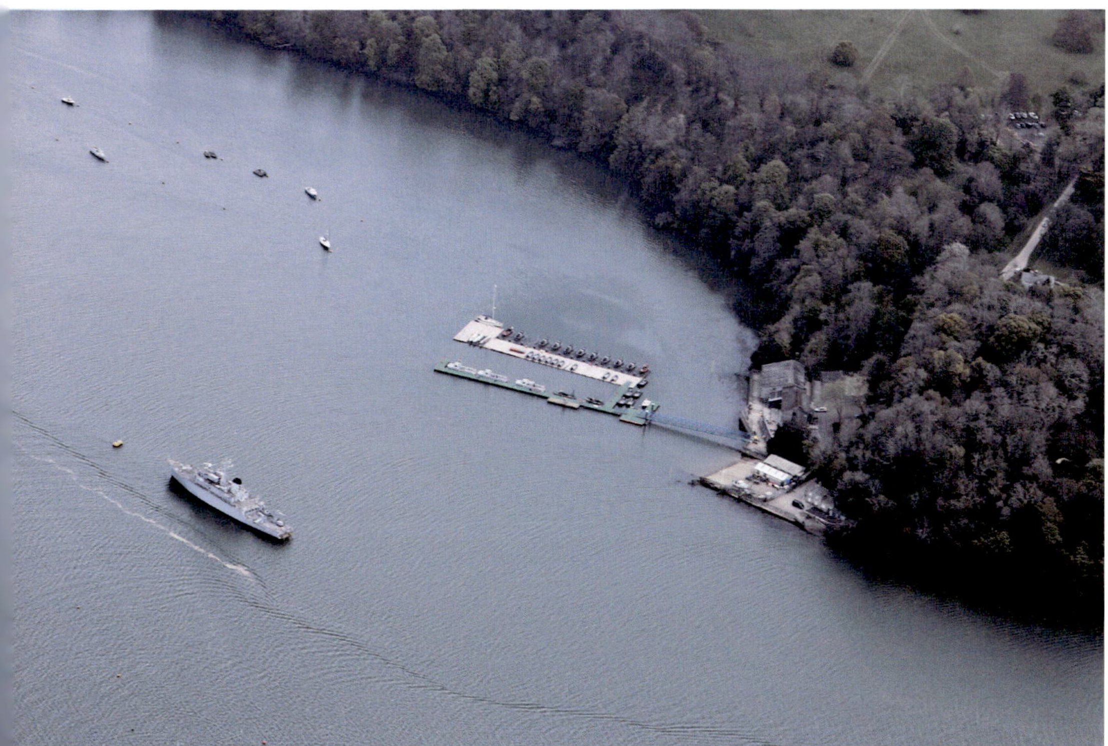

Jupiter Point.

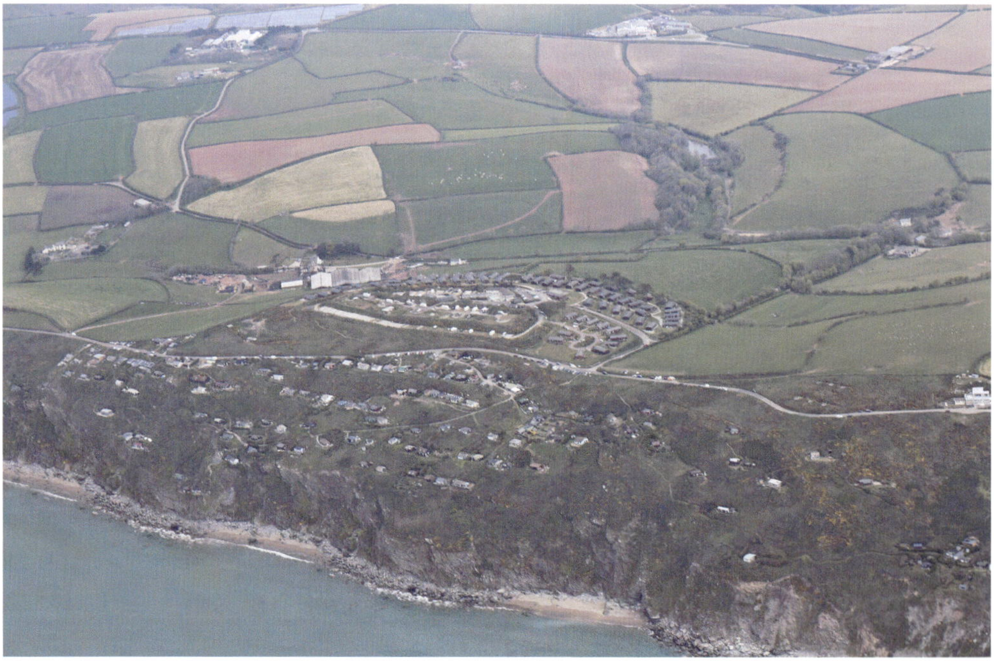

Whitsand Bay Battery, now a holiday park.

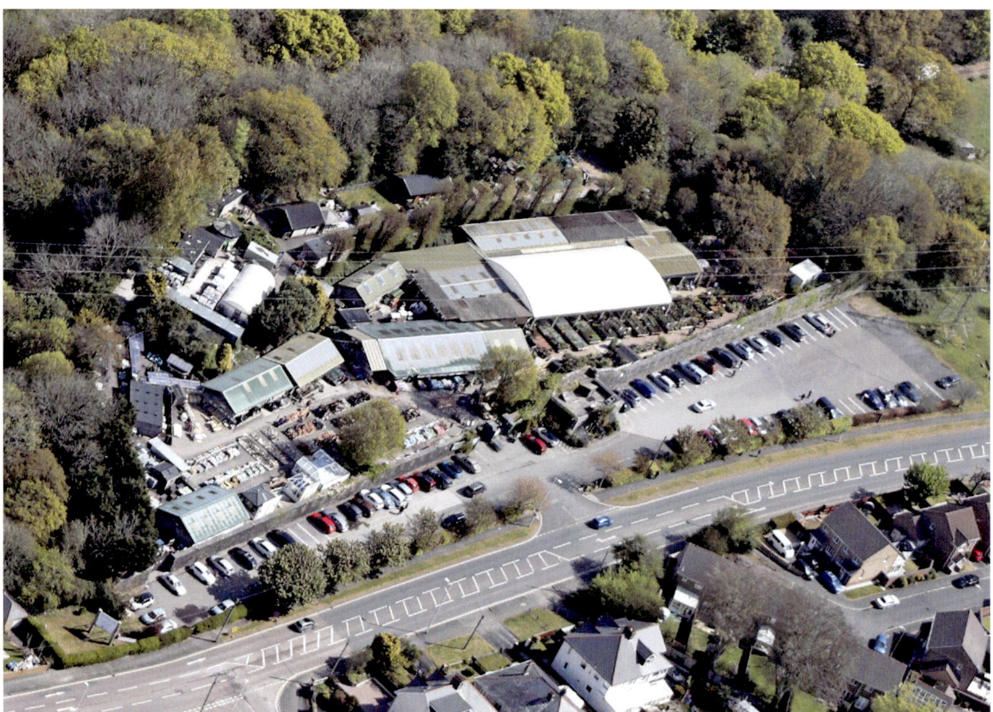

Bowden Battery, now a garden centre.

use. Fort Stamford is part residential and part caravan site. Laira Battery is now used for commercial operations. Polhawn Fort is a wedding venue.

Coypool

Has river and rail access. Opened in May 1941 as a depot for the Royal Electrical and Mechanical Engineers (REME). Its closure was announced in 1961. It then became home to 3 Commando Brigade Air Squadron from 1971 until the late 1990s. It is now a facility for Princess Yachts.

HMS *Cambridge*

This old holiday camp site on Wembury Point was commissioned as HMS *Cambridge* in 1956 as a naval gunnery school. Plymothians became used to the sound of gunfire in the Sound until the site was decommissioned in 2001. The site was purchased in 2006 by the National Trust and returned to nature, removing the gun mounts. It is now one of my favourite walks.

RM Turnchapel

The site became a Royal Marines base, Turnchapel, in 1993 and went on to become the home of 539 Assault Squadron RM equipped with various types of raiding craft and

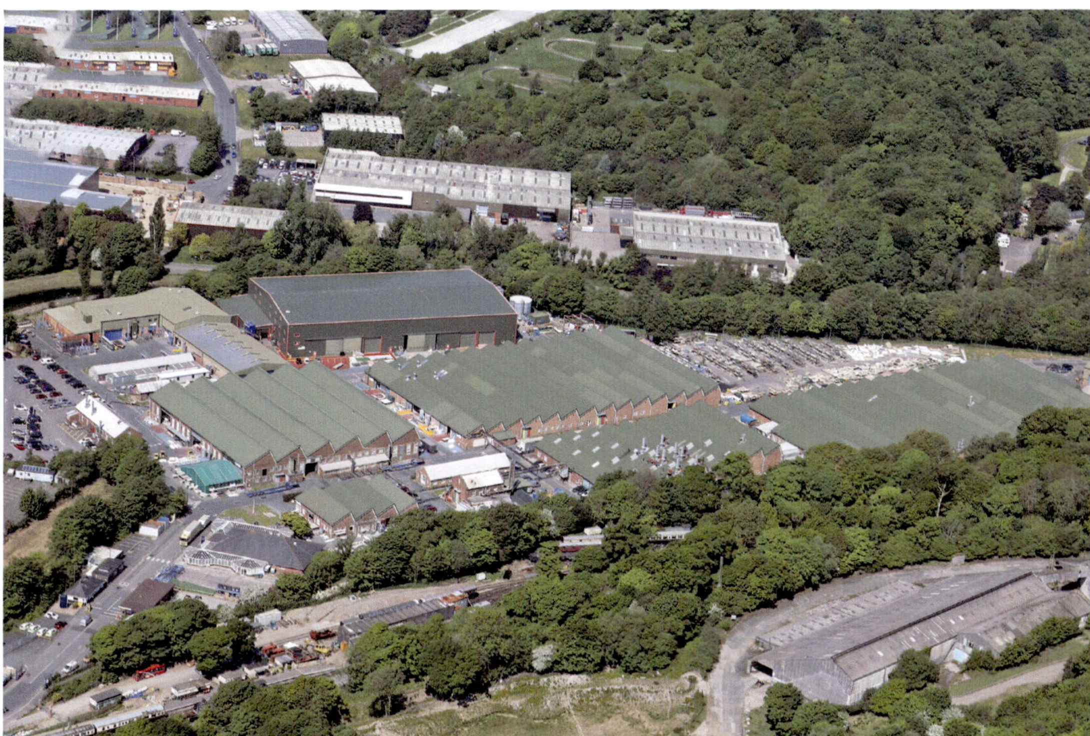

Coypool site.

vehicles, manned by over 100 Royal Marines and support personnel. It was also home to 10 Landing Craft Training Squadron. The site was sold off in 2013 and these units moved to RM Tamar.

RM Tamar

Based on the northern shore of Weston Mill Lake, just north of the old dockyard coaling wharf is RM Tamar, the base for the Royal Marines amphibious warfare ships. It handles both training and operations in landing craft, hovercraft and fast boats. The site was opened in 2013 by Prince Harry.

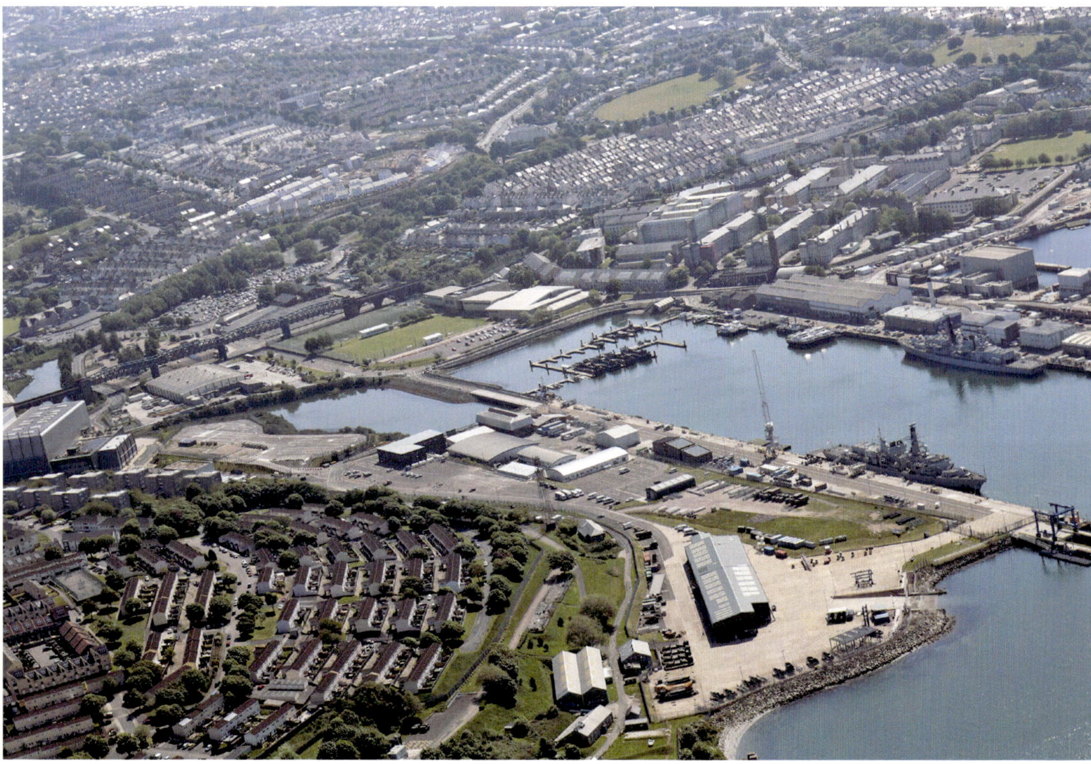

RM Tamar.